With pleasant memories of the
Fred McNeill family and
best wishes to you!

Maranda Cavanas Scoby

THE STORY OF CARTERVILLE:

ITS HUNDRED YEARS

1871-1971

LABAN CARTER
Co-founder of Carterville, on whose property coal was discovered.

THE STORY OF
CARTERVILLE:
ITS HUNDRED YEARS

1871-1971

MARANDA CAVANAS SCOBY

VANTAGE PRESS

NEW YORK   WASHINGTON   HOLLYWOOD

FIRST EDITION

Published by Vantage Press, Inc.
516 West 34th Street, New York, N. Y. 10001

Manufactured in the United States of America

Standard Book No. 533-00287-7

DEDICATED

to my maternal grandparents, W. E. Sizemore and Lucinda C. Sizemore, who planted the seed of loyalty to Carterville for their posterity. To my parents, William Sherman and Victoria Elizabeth Scoby, who left me a heritage of a love of my native town which is far greater than silver and gold.

ACKNOWLEDGMENTS

I am deeply appreciative of the numerous friends near and far who have given or sent to me choice bits and pieces of information to incorporate into my book. I also am sincerely grateful for the many people who have granted me personal interviews or given me old photographs relating to Carterville's early history. Each person who has so helped me I have endeavored to embody in the treatise as the story unfolded. To name each now individually would be repetition, and I feel there might be an unintentional oversight. Therefore, to each and all of them I say a big "Thank you." I express now particular thanks to Yvonne Jones for typing the entire manuscript, which she so kindly volunteered to do when the story was still in embryo form; and she has borne with me patiently at my own speed in getting it ready at intervals.

FOREWORD

"I'll do what I can." This statement expresses the philosophy by which Maranda Cavanas Scoby lives. It is also the usual reply one receives when requesting her aid in some matter needing attention. She gives freely whenever the request is within her ability to do so. She is a giver, seldom a receiver. And so now, she shares the reservoir of her memory by recalling episodes which were very much an integral part of the lives of the people of Carterville.

Too often, history is written to describe superficial, sensational events, neglecting the regularity and variation of daily life which gives to each individual the perseverance and diversity needed to prevail. Her book is devoted to human interest episodes of joys and sorrows that form much of the history of this small community and the lives of people who live and have lived here.

Should one ask Cavanas Scoby's friends to describe her, they would probably include a statement to the effect that she is a woman who has had three careers. While this statement is true, it is also limiting, for a career is the course one follows through life and Cavanas Scoby has followed many courses to reach her seventy-six years. Almost all of these courses have been directly associated with service toward others—a teacher for twenty-five years; a social-service worker for almost twenty years; a world traveller, to see and to learn; a participant in civic and community groups; a lifetime Christian and church worker; and, always a friend of children.

About thirty years ago during long, hot, humid, Sunday church services, the writer of this foreword first became acquainted with Cavanas Scoby in her continuing career as a friend of the child. The writer spent many delightful boyhood summers in Carterville with relatives who also attended the same church as did Cavanas Scoby. Never would we be accused of being "Backseat Baptist"; our seats were always up front near the pulpit. From this vantage point, I could usually watch in rapt fascination Cavanas Scoby's nimble fingers dance on the keyboard of the church organ. About the time the sermon began, my aunt or my grandmother would open one of their enchanting handbags. Pencils, paper pads, coloring books and other assorted noiseless delights would be revealed to my cousin and me. These materials usually held our attention unless the temperature was soaring. Then, as children will, about halfway through the sermon, we would begin to wiggle and squirm, perhaps in hopes that the movements would hurry the minister along to a successful conclusion. But, because of our competition with the ceiling fans, the wall fans, the funeral-home hand fans, and the general creaking of wooden pews as the congregation shifted positions, all of which contributed to the noise and motion of the church, our restlessness could hardly be noticed and our movements never distracted the minister. It was during those moments of restlessness that I would glance at Cavanas Scoby. She would smile, never frown in disapproval, and her smile assured me that the service was almost over. I would then sit quietly for the remaining time. Since that time long ago, I have wondered how many other children she quieted with her special smile.

The anonymous writer who wrote the following lines best describes the life of Maranda Cavanas Scoby.

> I expect to pass through this world but once. Any good, therefore, that I can do, or any kindness that I can show to any fellow creature, let me do it now. Let me not defer or neglect it, for I shall not pass this way again.

Keep writing, Cavanas Scoby—you have lots to tell. Your careers as public librarian and writer have just begun.

Marion, Illinois
July 1971   RONALD D. REED

INTRODUCTION

Memories are precious things, whether happy or sad. A small town known and loved in all its moods becomes woven into life's pattern and needs to be shared. Those born and reared in Carterville must have the greatest understanding of its people and their ways, its history with its homey human-interest stories, and its potentiality for future growth. As one who was born here just five years before the dawn of the twentieth century I have indeed put down roots and found contentment along the path of my native town's unique history. Thus the Story of Carterville is now recorded in my own method of a simple interpretation of its hundred years.

CONTENTS

THE STORY OF CARTERVILLE:

ITS HUNDRED YEARS

1871-1971

GEORGE MONROE McNEILL
Co-founder of Carterville and its first postmaster; picture taken after his return from the Civil War, 1865.

CHAPTER I

METAMORPHOSIS OF DIVISION STREET

Someone has said, "There is nothing so constant as change," and Division Street of Carterville is no exception. It was named by George M. McNeill, who laid out the original survey of the village from his forty-acre farm in 1871. It was his intention that this street become the town's main thoroughfare for business establishments—which it did.

He donated sixty feet off the eastern edge of his acreage, designating it "Division Street," hoping his adjacent farm neighbor on the east would give a similar width of ground which would therefore make this main street one-hundred-twenty feet wide, as he envisioned a broad avenue for a rapid growth of the new town. But his neighbor friend was unwilling to give any of his land for this purpose. The forty-acre plot extended from Grand Avenue on the south, to Anderson street on the north. Its western boundary he named Olive Street, for his first wife, who was Olive Herrin.

In due time, with coming business prospectors, McNeill's Original Survey, which was platted by William H. Bundy and Hezakiah L. Beasley, and recorded February 21, 1872, became the center of Carterville's merchandising section; and here is where the "metamorphosis," so to speak, began to burst open!

In 1878, Carterville was still in its infancy, and a forest stood where now substantial brick structures adorn Division Street. At that time there was only one small mine in the vicinity. Not many years later, other mines could be counted by the dozens. Five years after the first Carterville coal was shipped the first Elles Store was opened, in 1877, by Albert K. and Edward A. Elles, the founders.

17

It was located at the corner of Division Street and West Illinois Avenue in a small frame building, 20 x 40 feet. In 1885, the first large addition was made to their fast-growing business, consisting of two buildings, both frame, one a two-story 25 x 50 feet and the other 24 x 50 feet—the smaller one facing Division and the larger extending back of it on West Illinois. The large one a few years later was used as the store's barn, where the horses and delivery wagons utilized in the company's extensive delivery service were cared for and kept.

Buck Tygett, father of the late Emma Tygett, held this responsible job for a number of years. In the early 1900's George McGonagil was employed in this work, and has related how he worked many late hours putting up the team and wagon and feeding the horses after the store clerks had ended their day's work and gone home. This building later burned.

In 1891, the co-partnership was formed by the addition of two other Elles brothers, Louis and Charles. Two years later this company erected a large brick building facing Division. The date 1891 was in prominent view at the top. This impressive building, with its peaked cupola above the corner entrance, was an outstanding landmark on the street for many years and not so long ago was removed, due to the modern improvement of Heckel's Inc., which still occupies much of the original space, except the part on the original corner, now rented to Midtown Grocery.

Elles Store Company, as the firm was known after its enlargement, contained nine departments and was said to sell everything from needles to buggies, wagons, and even threshing machines in those early days; after the coming of the various models and makes of automobiles, the store became an agent for the "Star" and "Maxwell" cars. The business was built primarily upon the solid foundation of "Reliable Merchandise and Just Methods." Ila Franklin Beal has told me her father took care of the barn in the middle 1920's and the store sold Overland automobiles at that time. She was the recipient of one of these cars in 1929, holding the lucky number in a giveaway contest sponsored by this firm.

18

The first general store in the village was operated by the Carbondale Coal and Coke Company and run by John Herrin, Sr. It stood on the corner of Division and Virginia Avenue, later the site of the Thompson House, one of Carterville's early hotels. In 1884 F. C. and W. H. Zimmerman bought this store. "Charles and Henry"—as they were called—had worked with mine superintendent Bryden as bookkeepers. The Zimmerman Store was burned in the fire of 1898, but was reopened at once. A nice two-story brick, bearing the name ZIMMERMAN, next to the present Carterville State and Savings Bank, stands out as a reminder of these enterprising young business men.

A story has been handed down of timely interest about these energetic brothers, told by Merta Sonner, who knew them well. They innovated a "weather flag" after they came to Carterville, and it was hoisted each morning to tell the changes in weather. White flag was fair, then one was white and black, indicating unsettled; the back one of course meant stormy or bad weather.

Everyone in the new village depended on the "weather flag" flown on Division Street, since it could be seen near and far. A man named McCarthy had moved here from a southern state. He would get up, come outside to see the flag each morning and yell, "Hurrah for Jeff Davis!" and could be heard over the entire village. It gave everyone a good laugh.

But, let us go back to 1873. It was that year that Benjamin F. Tranbarger built a two-story house where the present drive-in bank is located, near the railroad that crosses Division at Grand Avenue, and opened the first independent grocery here —the store downstairs, living quarters up.

His daughter, Florence, who became Mrs. Will Dunston of Marion, Illinois had a millinery store just across Division from the grocery. Mr. Tranbarger operated his grocery until 1926, but in a different location in the business section.

A significant note can be inserted here. B. F.'s father, William Tranbarger, had a tobacco barn not far removed from the center of Division Street. In fact, it was situated where the

19

present housing project for the elderly is located, just east of Jones' Electric on East Illinois Avenue.

Tobacco was raised by a number of the early farmers, who had pioneered here from Kentucky and Tennessee on land that later was included in the corporation limits. At this barn, tobacco was cured, dried and pressed down in hogsheads, then transported to Metropolis to ship on the Ohio River.

William Tranbarger's daughter, Alice, who later became the second Mrs. George McNeill, worked in his barn-factory making cigars. Alice Tranbarger was Carterville's first woman schoolteacher, in its first school, in 1873, held in Brown's Boarding House, a short distance off Division Street, which stood at the corner of East Grand and Pennsylvania Avenue.

As to be expected in a new village getting started business-wise in those early days, the first stores were built of wood. According to a historical account by J. F. Wilcox, published in 1905 "the city (Carterville) has been visited by very destructive fires four times—the first in March 1885, then in April 1897; August 1898 and August 1900. But it was practically rebuilt with brick." The same writer also goes on to say: "The following is pretty nearly a complete list of the industries of the city at the present time (1905)—Five general stores, one hardware, two clothing, six restaurants, one electric light plant, three lumber yards, five barber shops, two blacksmith shops, one photography gallery, two drug stores, two shoe shops, two livery stables, two feed stables, two tailor shops, one bakery, one jewelry store, one harness shop, two millinery stores, two butcher shops, five grocery stores, two hotels, one furniture and exchange store, one laundry (Chinese), two furniture and undertaking rooms, one cigar factory, two boarding houses, one weekly newspaper, nine saloons, one cornet band (Gunster's), two dentists, three lawyers, one surveying and engineering company, four insurance agents, two printing offices, four resident ministers, four physicians, and one flouring mill."

In reference to the big fire in 1898 the following authenticated news is given as it appeared in the *Carterville Tribune* (published by Clarence Bush) of August 23, 1898; "Twenty-six buildings in ash. Losses amount to over $70,000. The scene of the early morning conflagration at Carterville on Monday is a sad one to behold. From the 1. C. Railroad on the south to Illinois Avenue on the north, only one building escaped destruction. The places of the frame buildings are marked only by a heap of smoking debris, while the walls of the brick buildings are still standing, a desolate sentinel of the once beautiful business houses.

"The fire was first discovered in the building occupied by J. M. Lauder, as a saloon. In less than an hour almost thirty buildings were consumed, while about thirty five firms were burned out of business.

"True to the hustling and enterprising spirit which has always been a leading characteristic of our village, permits were issued last night for temporary buildings, while contracts have already been let for permanent business houses, and in a few months Carterville will have risen from her ashes stronger and better than ever before.

F. C. Zimmerman and Brothers loss on stock and building, $15,800, insurance $9,600.

J. L. Gallimore, attorney, library loss $200, insurance $100.

G. Bush, Carterville Tribune, loss $1,700, insurance $650.

George E. Clark and Wife, building and stock, loss $1,000, insurance $575.

James Thompson, building loss $1,000, insurance $700.

Ben L. Washburn, building loss $4,100, insurance $1,800.

Warren Walker, stock $7,000, insurance $5,000.

A. C. Hope, building and machinery, $3,000, insurance $500.

W. C. Lofland, stock $400, fully covered.

T. W. Cotrell, physician, furniture, etc., $100, fully covered.

Moake and Impson, stock and building $7,000, insurance $4,000.

Mrs. S. E. Hancock, buildings $1,500, insurance $400.

George Bayless, stock and building $1,000, insurance $400.

G. H. Bundy, building $200, insurance $150.

B. H. Carter, building and stock $3,700, insurance $2,950.

J. W. Vick, furniture, etc., $600, insurance $300.

J. J. Hunter, building and stock $2,200, insurance $1,600.

Jeff Cox, building and stock $2,200, insurance $1,200.

R. Adler, stock $2,000, insurance $1,000.

I. M. Walker, building $3,000, insurance $1,550.

M. C. Barnett, building $500, fully covered.

W. J. Walker, feed stable $100, covered.

J. M. Lauder, stock $200, no insurance.

B. F. Copeland, building and furniture $2,500, insurance $500.

V. W. Williams, household furniture $250, no insurance.

Bank of Carterville, building and fixtures $2,000, no insurance.

Peter Jeffrey, building $3,000, insurance $200.

Mrs. Lavender, stock $300, no insurance

and J. E. Entsminger, dental instruments $250.00.

"There were several accidents during the fire. Several people were on the roof of the building of F. C. Zimmerman and Brothers, when an explosion occured caused by the accumulation of gas. Among those injured were: Arch Adams, Dick Kelley, Ves Eveland, W. B. Keith, and a Mr. Richardson. A few other men were in the accident whose names were not printed in the report."

In discussing this printed account of that tragic fire with Mrs. Lina North and her sister, Ruth Bracy, here recently, they both told the writer they remembered it vividly. Being young girls at that time they ran from the Park Hotel (which their father owned) on South Division Street as near to Elles Store as they could get. The volunteer firemen in a bucket brigade were climbing up and down the ladders set against that large store, fighting hard to save it—which they did. They recalled that Mrs. Lavender had a fashionable millinery near the front entrance in the store. They also said that W. B. Keith was their brother-in-law, the husband of their late sister "Little Molly" Keith, who resided with Lina prior to her death in 1968.

It has just been learned, too, that Thomas Richardson, Sr., who is now Carterville's oldest citizen, and his brother, Joke, both in their nineties, were among those courageous and noble firefighters that day. According to Thomas' statement to his daughter, Jennie V. Winter, "Joke" received an injury to his leg while they were trying to save the burning Elles Store building. There were no neighboring fire departments to come to assist them and they obtained water from neighborhood wells, even using wet blankets to try to smother the blazes.

But like the fabled "Phoenix," Division Street was destined to rise from the ashes and be more progressive than ever. A city ordinance was promptly passed that no frame buildings could be erected as business places in the future, but had to be built with brick.

It was in 1884 that J. V. Walker founded a men's clothing store at the corner of the village "square" where Division Street intersected Illinois Avenue. It was destined to become the "mother store" of a chain of eleven other similar establishments in Southern Illinois in the early 1900's, branching out into the state of Ohio in 1928 with four other stores—these stores known as J. V. Walker and Son's Clothing Stores.

J. V., known as "Vince," had three sons, Fred, Carl and Jo, whom he had capably trained in the establishment. At the time of the founding (1884) J. V. and his brother, Warren, were partners in a combination clothing and grocery store; but they later dissolved partnership and Warren Walker continued to sell groceries, adding dry goods and shoes to his stock at a separate building farther down on the east side of South Division. No doubt this first clothing store was constructed of wood, and when it was rebuilt, after the tragic fire, brick was used.

There was a brick kiln run by Sam Henderson, not far distant behind North Division where Anderson Street joins Hickory, that did a flourishing business manufacturing bricks

23

for the new brick business-buildings, as well as shipping thousands on the railroad. The old Burr mine switch that crossed North Division ran right by the kiln plant, and there was the Dump Pond nearby. This pond furnished a fine recreation sport in the winter for the young people's skating parties, especially on Sunday afternoons.

In summer the smaller children derived much fun in making "mud pies" and miniature bricks out of the soft clay for their playhouses. The pond's major importance, of course, was the kiln's water supply. Even today young boys like to pillage at its site to explore for things dumped there in years gone by. Only recently John Flora, a postal employee, while exploring there found a small glass medicine bottle with these words molded in it: "S. H. Bundy, Druggist. Carterville, Illinois." An old published account of the Carterville Brick Company owned by S. H. Bundy, F. W. Richart and C. E. Owens, states that the plant had a capacity of 25,000 bricks daily and employed fifteen men. Ruth Hampton Washburn, daughter of R. H. H. Hampton, founder of Hampton Drug Company, has told the writer that some few years prior to its founding, S. H. Bundy had a drug store on the southeast corner of Illinois and Division where her father later established his drugstore business. In 1906, Mr. Hampton moved from that location to the present one at 112 North Division. Dr. W. H. Perry had owned the business before S. H. Bundy bought it. Bundy in 1904 became the bank's first president.

The late George Lockie related to the writer about five years ago how as a twelve-year-old lad he had helped manufacture the bricks that were used to construct the big two-story J. V. Walker building that is still a landmark on the "square." The lower story housed the men's and boy's furnishings, and the Odd Fellows' Hall was above.

An amusing story has been revealed just lately as told to Forrest Hampton by Jo Walker, a son of J. V., exemplifying the aggressiveness in early advertising and super-salesmanship of "Vince" Walker. A large wooden box of boys' red caps had been delivered to the store by Bennie Smith, the drayman, direct from the I. C. Railroad depot. Mr. Walker called in a young lad, possibly nine or ten years old, and asked him to help him open the box. The lad did, and for his pay he gave him one of the red caps. The child was naturally elated and ran out wearing his new scarlet cap, and in no time at all other boys flocked to the store for similar caps. Soon the entire box was completely sold out. It was then that Division Street was spectacular and conspicuous with proud urchins wearing their brilliant flame headgear.

There is also an item of interest relating to the three white links that can still be seen embedded in the recessed brick-walled center window in the front of the upper story of the Walker building. Many present-day residents will remember them but perhaps do not know their history. There is quite an interesting story as to their origin.

Leo Watson, who was widely known as a cashier for fifty years in the Carterville State and Savings Bank, and also for his service as a Carterville Community High School board member for many years, related to the writer just a few months before his death in 1968 a historical slant about these three links, symbol of the I.O.O.F.

He stated that his father, E. B. Watson, then mayor of the town, whose hobby was making canes of various woods and leather, carved the links from cypress; and they were painted white and placed in the brick masonry. Mayor Watson, himself an Odd Fellow, was a member of the I.O.O.F. here, which was instituted in Carterville on February 17, 1882 by Judge George W. Young of Marion, with a membership of one hundred seventy-five.

J. V. Walker's new two-story brick building originally had a corner entrance similar to that of Elles Store Company, and also the Carterville State and Savings Bank, before it was remodeled, as did the fourth important brick structure known as the Joe E. Kelly Drug Store on the southeast corner of the "square." It was about 1906 that Kelley, a young druggist, started his drug store on that prominent corner where the streetcar rails terminated; and he was a dealer in wallpaper, paints, oils and glass. A small glass bottle was found recently by John Watson, superintendent of the Carterville City and Water Department, bearing the name "Joe E. Kelley, Druggist, Carterville, Illinois" molded in the glass. It was turned up in recent excavation by Mr. Watson on East Illinois Avenue.

Grace Kelley, after her druggist husband's death, married a Mr. Graham and operated a well-patronized confectionery on the same corner. It was a favorite rendezvous where the stylish of the town could meet to learn the latest news of the day or simply share small-town gossip while perchance waiting for the incoming streetcar at that corner. So it was that J. V. Walker's Store, Kelley's Drug Store, the Carterville State and Savings Bank and the Elles Store Company, each with their imposing and matching corner entrances with a single column in front of their double-door entries, bounded the city's business square.

There were stepping-stones between and connecting each. Many a fashionably dressed woman wearing high-top lace or button pointed-toed shoes with high heels and ankle-length narrow skirts in the vogue of that day, had difficulty in maneuvering their footsteps over these stones, especially in muddy weather. The black gumbo streets were unpaved, and it was not until 1910 that the concrete sidewalks were built along the principal streets of the town. The Lough Construction Company, Marion, was the contractor.

I must mention a unique feature inside the J. V. Walker building at the rear. It was a large barber shop equipped with the three up-to-date barber chairs and six or eight "waiting chairs." There was even a water keg with a faucet in one corner and also a convenient spittoon on the inlaid linoleum floor covering. George Watkins, Malcom Sims and Tommy Council, barbers, are shown in a picture with John McNeil, the Reverend R. O. Rodgers, pastor of the Christian Church, and Dr. J. W. Vick, customers, in the year 1909. The barber pole just outside the double-door entrance facing Illinois Avenue and the streetcar line advertised "Baths." So it catered to a high-class barber trade.

Adjoining Walker's on the north was "The Model" Confectionery, owned by X. M. Huss, a noted candy-maker, as well as an expert in the making of ice creams, concocting sodas and other confections.

Perry Sizemore, a popular high-school lad, by his after-school work there as a "soda jerk" became known as "Jerker," a nickname which he has borne since about 1912 until now. He resides now in San Clemente, California not far from President Nixon's home. During depression days this confectionery bore the sweet name "Sugar Bowl" and was under the management of Dillard and Ina Underwood.

Of special importance was the well-patronized butcher shop owned by W. W. Snyder and James Phillips. The present Carterville Herald Office occupies the building. All meats sold by them were slaughtered at the Henry Phillips farm at the northwest edge of town. Henry was the father of James and was skilled in making pressed meats, stuffing sausages and smoking them as well as bacon and hams. He had learned this trade as a native of Germany before coming to this country. Back of the building was a high board fence that enclosed the smoke houses and the equipment to prepare the various kinds of meat for market. Both Snyder and his partner were experienced cattle buyers, also, and it was said they could easily have become rich had they established a meat-packing plant with their know-how before the turn of the twentieth century. Later H. W. Bateman and the Briggeman brothers and also John Visconti were proprietors of the butcher shop at the same stand.

On the same side of the street a decade or so before 1900 near the corner of Jersey Street stood "The Apothecary Shop" owned by Dr. Price, whose face was framed with neatly cropped short black beard and equally black, glossy hair, a bit long but always trimly cut, which gave him the appearance of a character depicted from a Charles Dickens novel. "Old Doc" Price, as he was called, endeared himself to the children, it was said, with his handouts of sweetly perfumed advertising cards, and his shop was stocked with fine perfumes sold by the gram.

On this corner in 1905, the First National Bank was situated, having been organized that year with Albert K. Elles as president and Dr. H. V. Ferrell as vice president. A. J. Guerrattaez was the first cashier and Mike Ferrell, the doctor's son, succeeded him in 1910. This new bank was the first business to occupy the new K. P. brick building. Next to it on the south was the Hampton Drug Store in the Hampton Building erected in 1906. The same year it moved to its fine new quarters with its massive and beautiful soda fountain and very up to date interior fixtures. And of course the very best line of patent medicines, also prescriptions by a very qualified, licensed pharmacist, Chat Hampton, son of the owner R. H. H. Hampton.

In 1919, the First National Bank moved to the former Joe E. Kelley building. In the spring of 1930 it was a victim of the Depression, with the rest of the banks in Williamson County that closed all in the same day. A very sad day that was for Carterville and the other neighboring towns!

Probably the most outstanding large brick building that grips more attention of newcomers to the town today on North Division is the J. B. Samuel, with the date 1897 on the upper story. Mr. Samuel actually started in the lumber business with a capital of one hundred-twenty dollars in 1885 when Carterville was only fourteen years old. The upstairs of the present building as we see it today was the Opera House, with quite a large stage and opera seats that catered to high-class legitimate plays and vaudeville on regular circuit. It was considered a real treat to attend the "opera" and perchance view a real melodrama. The huge curtains, and they were beautifully painted, were pulled up and down usually by middle-size boys whose pay for doing this service was seeing the ongoing of the fascinating show. I well remember in 1910 the Carterville eighth-grade and high-school graduates held their first joint commencement exercises in this building. Standing out in my memory is the fainting of one of the three high-school girls in that class while she was delivering her oration.

It was a requisite of the high school in those days that each graduate must write, memorize and deliver an oration to earn a diploma. These joint commencements continued through 1916. At the 1914 graduation exercises, the honored high-school class of fourteen graduates, the largest class up until that time, were seated on the stage with the school board members behind them, all erect in spindled-back wooden chairs facing the audience. Each boy graduate was to give an oration; the rules had been altered, allowing the eight girls to perform with music solos or duets, even though they had each written an oratory essay. The six boys wore black tuxedos (rented). One board member, Fred Walker of the J. V. Walker store, and Snyder S. Vick, founder of the Vick Drug Company, another member, were heard to remark that they could scarcely refrain from tying the boy's frock-tail coats to their chairs before they went forward to stand to deliver their speeches. I am sure havoc and hilarious laughter would have ensued if these two board members had carried out their "hunch."

Besides Mr. Samuel's lumber office downstairs, the adjoining north room was occupied by the Carterville Store Company that was begun in 1898 by the young, ambitious owners, Willard and Oscar Peyton. It was sometimes called the "Cash Store," selling groceries, dry goods and shoes. Early in the 1920's a Miner's Cooperative Store selling miner's supplies in addition to the aforesaid merchandise had a going business there for some time.

The building is now used for the Eagle's Lodge. Adjoining on the ground floor is "The Antique," owned by Mayor Frank Samuel, Jr., and William Humphreys. This small addition formerly housed "The Modern Cleaners," operated by John and Helen Peach, and afterwards the "Kozy Kitchen" lunch room.

During 1900-1904 Carterville nearly doubled its population. In 1887 there were one thousand inhabitants here. The village was chartered with three hundred inhabitants, according to a petition with thirty-six signatures, sworn to and approved April 10, 1872 by J. A. Bandy and George M. McNeill. However, a post office had been secured by transferring the old office of Fredonia to the town site, which was renamed Carterville on December 8, 1871, and George M. McNeill was the first postmaster.

Many of the merchants, mine and land owners became stockholders in the Carterville State and Savings Bank. About thirty-five of the hustling promoters of Carterville's best interets, representing the wealthiest and most influential citizens of the city and county, organized this bank, which opened its doors for business on April 12, 1904, on the east side of the street just south of Vick's Drug Store—the building last occupied by Loise Dress Shop. Samuel H. Bundy became president, J. B. Samuel, vice president (later served as president several years), and M. W. Sizemore, cashier. Leo E. Watson was added to the personnel as assistant cashier after completion of his business courses at Gem City Business College, Quincy, in 1907. Today he is memorialized by a beautiful bronze plaque of his likeness, which is just inside the present bank entrance, in honor of his fifty years' service with the bank, Williamson County's Oldest.

As early as 1883, a newspaper was published in the village by John H. Barton, but only a few issues and no record of names available; the plant moved to Creal Springs. Actually, Carterville's first newspaper, known as the *Tribune,* was begun in 1892 by James P. Copeland, who sold it to Clarence Bush in 1898, who in turn sold it to L. E. Robertson in 1900. This editor changed its name to the *Herald.*

Location of Copeland's press was on South Division Street about where Hayton's Threatre stood in the 1940's, on the spot that is now occupied by the Modernell Beauty Shop. Due to burn-out, the press was moved to the Belford Building on North Division Street across from Hampton Drug Store.

Mr. Robertson soon moved into a building known as the old printing shop that stood at the corner of East Illinois and Pennsylvania Avenue, just two blocks off Division. L. E. Robertson was the father of the late Mrs. A. G. (Ruth) Heckel. In 1917, C. S. Coddington bought the paper and the business was moved into the K. of P. building next to Hampton's, where it remained for many years—Frank Ledbetter buying it in 1923, and published it until 1958, when he sold out and moved to Nevada, Iowa.

After a period of several years, the *Carterville Herald,* now under the new ownership of Davison Publication since July 1969, is fast gaining due recognition through its subheading: "Home of Two Colleges," giving pertinent news that actually is of timely interest to the surrounding areas it is serving. As of March 1, 1971 the publishers renamed it *Williamson County Observer,* with its new slogan, "A community newspaper for the people of Williamson County"—continuing the *Herrin Spokesman, Carterville Herald* and *Johnston City Progress.*

Another news medium came to Carterville in 1899. It was the first telephone exchange, a home-made one by Howard Munger from Carbondale. According to Merta McNeil Sonner, it had twenty-five little square drops that were made of copper, and when a patron rang his telephone, a drop fell to attract the attention of the telephone girl.

The exchange was first located in the Hampton Drug Store on the corner of Division and East Illinois, where the clerks took care of it. The late Miss Tena Thompson had the first custody of it—or, as we would now designate, she was "the telephone girl," for she was clerk in that drug store. Later a telephone operator was hired to receive and transmit calls, and for nothing else. And who was the first operator? "It happened to be Miss Merta McNeill!" (These are Merta's actual words.)

One notable quote Merta has written to the writer is as follows: "The billing of cars of coal shipped from No. 7 mine at Herrin went through this telephone office each day the mine worked. Gussie Newkirk would give the billing to the head office in Carbondale. One of the saddest things in my life happened here while listening to Gussie. She told Mr. Wilson in the Carbondale office they had an accident. He asked if anyone was hurt. She wouldn't answer and he asked the third time. She said "Yes" and told his name. It was my brother, Arthur, the one born the year Carterville started, 1871. She knew I was listening. We all cried. It gave me a shock I never will outlive." Thus, this link with the past early local telephone history is a fresh reminder of the many mine tragedies experienced in the booming little mining town in the years that followed.

There is on record a city ordinance passed and approved April 6, 1903 (E. B. Watson, Mayor) granting that the Williamson and adjoining Counties' Telephone Company be authorized to erect, operate and maintain a telephone system or exchange in the City of Carterville. So this unique and amazing system of communication was soon available to local residents; and people all over town as well as in the adjacent rural areas were installing house telephones, the long box-like wall models so popular then, which today are considered collector's items.

With crank telephones being installed even over the immediate rural areas, reaching out to the many farmers who came to do their weekly "trading" at Carterville's numerous stores, news traveled fast. Many patrons were connected on the same party line, sometimes eight to ten on a line; and to contact any given party the phone would ring in codes of "longs and shorts." Each person on the line knew everyone else's phone-code ring, and if one preferred to eavesdrop, which many did, several could listen in on the news or gossip at one time; and they often butted in, too.

Edna Spires Travis tells a true story of a hired hand, Will Frye, who worked on her father's farm at the edge of town. This fellow was quite adept playing any tune by ear, that anyone might mention, on his Jew's harp. So it wasn't uncommon after the farm chores were done to have someone call John Spires and ask to have Will play "Red Wing," "The Good Old Summer Time," "In the Shade of the Old Apple

Tree," or other well-known popular tunes of that day. Numerous party-liners made request after request, which pleased the simple-hearted Will no end! Thus many householders with their receivers clicking down were furnished a whole evening's Jew's-harp entertainment. The rural party line became known as the "Hay Seed Line."

Directly across the street from Hampton Drug Store was the Belford building, a two-story brick affair pretentious with the name of the owner in white and its upstairs porch with iron-grill railing and posts from roof to sidewalk. It had been built for Frank Belford, a saloon proprietor during that period prior to the turn of this century when there were numerous saloons in town. Some years after the saloons were voted out the lower story was occupied by the popular cleaning shop of Evan Phillips. He and his pretty young wife, Dorothy, lived in the upstairs apartments. Janice Lockie, now Mrs. William Searl, Sr., also maintained in the front section of the lower floor one of the first "Beauty Parlors" established in our town. That was in the days when "marcel waves" with electric curling irons were the most modern equipment for the up-to-date hair-do! Bobbed hair was just then becoming fashionable too. There had also been a restaurant in the building run by Mr. and Mrs. E. W. Coss, later operated by Terry and Kate Carter. The Belford building later burned.

Just south was that portion of Elles Store Company known as the queensware department, also the furniture and hardware sections. The queensware shelves were well stocked with beautiful fine china, much of it imported and handpainted. There were also fine glassware such as cut glass and patterns of silver service, all of which would be considered conversation pieces on the antique market today or valuable heirlooms. The finest quality of furniture were no less treasured items in many of our early homes. Folding beds, both upright and mantel type, and beautiful massive sideboards were much in demand at that time.

Between the hardware and clothing departments of the store was a building housing H. W. Cann's book and music

33

store. Mr. Cann also sold school supplies as well as candy, and he stocked the most beautiful fancy valentines of pink celluloid, actual replicas of banjos and violins that would gladden the heart of any maiden for whom they were purchased. He loved children and would give them delicious "yellow jackets" and "candy kisses" with their purchases. He had been postmaster of Carterville in 1896 and 1897 when the post office was located south of Dr. Perry's office on South Division Street, now occupied by the Tiny Tot Shop.

Adjoining Cann's Store on the south was the Thompson saloon, in the northeast corner of which was a small separate room fronting North Division. This was Frank Sizemore's barber shop, established in 1891, with its unique lettered sign on the entrance, "U-R NEXT." Some years later he moved his shop, designating it then as "Shaving Parlor," to the Washburn Building on the west side of South Division, where he continued his business for more than fifty years. Andy's Bakery now occupies this spot. Sizemore had an old cupboard in the back of his shop which was used in the days of the handlebar mustache, to keep the shaving mugs of regular customers. Each mug had the customer's name in gold letters on it. Some of the mugs bore the following names: James Armstrong, merchant; Dr. H. V. Ferrell; Ben Washburn, merchant and postmaster; M. Wilson Sizemore, banker; Leon Crain, merchant; V. Rice, druggist; William Bauman, depot agent; E. W. Coss, cafe operator; William Briggeman, W. W. Snyder and M. T. Bateman, all butchershop proprietors; Charley Owens, jeweler; and A. K. Elles and Ed Elles, merchants.

It is timely to note at this point in my story that several years after Frank Sizemore's death in 1958 the shaving mug bearing M. W. Sizemore's name in gold with the date 1898 was located in a junk antique shop east of Johnston City and was purchased there by the late Zella Sizemore Scott, the daughter of this prominent banker who was the first cashier of the Carterville State and Savings Bank.

An article published several years ago in the *Carterville Herald* tells of an interview Editor Frank Ledbetter held with

Frank Sizemore in his "shaving parlor," in which Sizemore stated that when he started barbering in 1891 there were no telephones. He recalled that Marion (Shay) Stocks, who was working with him, rigged up a communications system of wire from Sizemore's house to his barber shop with tin cans and reflectors at each end so Mr. and Mrs. Sizemore could talk to each other. At that time the genial barber and wife resided in a cottage where Holmes Garage now stands. Thus novel methods of communication were of interest "way back then!"

Also a timely story relating to Frank Sizemore and his great love for music tells that, before the turn of the century the Bryden Coal Company, interested in organizing a Carterville band, bought instruments for a band started by Leo Gunster. Gunster left Carterville and the Sizemore Concert Band succeeded it in 1897. Sizemore, its conductor, played his clarinet with the band for fifty-eight consecutive years at the Williamson County Fair. A letter sent to the writer by Josie Gunster Cash of Charleston, West Virginia some months ago mentions that her brother, Leo Gunster, traveled several years all over the country with famed Barnum and Bailey Circus band. It is reasonable to assume that he left our town for the luring adventure to join this great circus in its heyday.

The Thompson Building, in which the saloon was located, consisted of two stories. Above the saloon was the large UMWA hall where the miners met regularly. The United Mine Workers of America Union had come into being about 1898. Sizemore's Band held their yearly Thanksgiving celebrations and election of officers there for a number of years, but conducted regular practices in the Old City Hall. Helen Harris Peach tells how she and neighboring playmates loved to hear it practicing and would dance around on the outside in front of the hall. The Harris family lived next door west. She also recalls peeping in the barred windows of the City Hall's basement, then the town's jail, most generally called the "calaboose," to gaze in at the prisoners while her mother took the meals to those incarcerated there. Mrs. Harris was paid by the city for this service. The barred windows are still there, but no one has been jailed in it for a number of years.

Merta Sonner in a letter to me some time ago posed this question: "I wonder who remembers the high sidewalk or bridge that extended from the I. C. Railroad crossing on South Division to about where Frost's Furniture Store is now?"

She stated it was built about 1886 and began to rise at the railroad, and in going over Pin Oak branch (in Division's low hollow) the bridge was so high a man could easily walk under it. She further stated that Pin Oak branch was in the barn lot of the George M. McNeill farm, the home being the first hotel in Carterville.

Well, believe it or not, I have found two Carterville native ladies who remember this historic bridge, namely, Lina North and her sister, Ruth Bracy. They recall it was three planks wide and had high bannisters on both sides. Both affirm that when their first-born sons, George North and William Layne Bracy, were babies they would practice rolling each of their baby buggies along the high walk-way trying to keep the cart wheels from getting stuck in the cracks. This was probably around 1903 or 1904. They further emphasized that they remembered running over the bridge to the big fire of 1898, when the volunteer fireman were working so desperately to save Elles' Store.

They recalled, too, that their father, Charles Cash, at the time of this great fire, was clerking in the Zimmerman Brothers Store. The name Zimmerman high on the front of that building is another reminder today of Carterville's merchant princes in those early days.

Pin Oak went on a spring binge every year for many years. Many residents still living here can remember when it would overflow to such an extent that water flooded many of the business places at such times, and also would back up, covering Walnut Street a short distance behind South Division.

But it is good now to know that this unruly stream (that actually begins a mere brook behind the Christian Science

Church) has been harnessed with large underground tiling under Division's concrete pavement. It still meanders over much of its former course; and when at last it bends southward under a concrete bridge on West Grand Avenue, it is a veritable creek. Then it wends on south past our Oakwood Cemetery, until it empties into beautiful Crab Orchard Lake. No one apparently knows when the old wooden bridge on Division was torn away.

Suffice it to say, the city built its concrete sidewalks in 1910. That, I myself remember.

Just across the old high sidewalk bridge and over the double tracks of the Illinois Central Railroad that crossed Division at its intersection with Grand Avenue at the south end of the main business section was a very important manufacturing concern that had its beginning in 1894, just four years prior to the very disastrous fire that leveled the greater portion of the town's business establishments. But fortunately the tall, large building, three stories in height, escaped the holocaust.

This was the Colp-Arnold Flouring Mill founded by John Colp and his friend Hezekiah F. Arnold. These two gentlemen had had much experience in the field of wheat-threshing, as well as selling all kinds of heavy machinery, so were well qualified to handle and deal in grain—which at that time was a most promising business.

They had also been in the sawmill business, cutting much lumber out of the forests that abounded in this area and in Missouri in the 1870's and 1880's. Don't forget that many large trees were still in the "forest cocoon" of Carterville!

With this background of knowledge and experience they erected the millage firm of Colp-Arnold Company of Carterville (also known as Carterville Milling Company) that became a very active factor in the industrial life of the community; and they built up a business of considerable magnitude, operating a hundred-barrel mill together with handling and dealing in grain.

Mr. Colp came to Carterville community in 1876 and purchased a farm on Eight Mile Prairie, just one-and-one half miles west of the young village. The homestead is now occupied by his son and wife, Mr. and Mrs. Logan N. Colp, and Eight Mile Prairie is now filled with many new homes, which no doubt in the future will be included in the corporation area of our town. The Main Street in this new residential area bears the historic name "Eight Mile Prairie Road."

H. F. Arnold, known as "Uncle Hez," wore a long beard, was quite religious and had an uncanny shrewdness in monetary matters that designated him as a real financier. His partner, John Colp, was nonetheless shrewd in all business considerations; and both of these outstanding gentlemen built up a sound milling business, known far and wide.

The late Harve North was the first miller working for this firm, until his marriage in 1901. His widow, Lina North, has given me some delightful information about this mill. It manufactured a high quality of flour under the brand name "Purity," much of which was shipped to other towns by train. The I.C.R.R. tracks skirted the large mill on the east with a convenient siding spur.

Joe Ellis, father of Ida Jeffery, Herrin, served as fireman and custodian of the machinery. Mrs. North has told how Mr. Ellis also had the responsibility of sounding the old steam fire whistle when a blaze was reported, and this whistle was very loud and shrill. On New Year's Eve each year it would blow for a long time.

Joe Stocks also worked there and liked to tease the young girls when he was all covered with the white flour. The mill also ground a good grade of corn meal which Mrs. Morrisy, a neighbor, purchased by the five-cent bag every day, declaring as she was returning home just back of the Park Hotel (operated by Charlie Cash, father of Mrs. North) that it was "such good meal."

Charles Butts, our City Clerk, told me an interesting item on February 26, 1970, as I was observing the wrecking of the old brick garage behind the library (formerly the old City Hall.) I noticed its six half-windows of arched brick and a doorway on the west side that was concreted up. As we were looking through the back glass door of the library, I asked, "Could this building have been an early jail?" He replied, "It was not a jail but was the old fire-engine house." Mr. Butts went on to say he remembered as a lad when his father was head of the fire department and the engine was drawn by two big horses. Whenever the fire whistle sounded its loud, shrill siren at the mill, these steeds, like old war horses, were rarin' to go. When the engine was to be returned the horses needed no guidance with their reins but, reaching the corner of West Illinois Avenue at the bank, turned there and made the correct turn and another turn left, stopping abruptly at the engine house. So it was that this unique old building was completely demolished in March, 1970, and another Carterville landmark, not without its significance, is now history.

Succeeding Harve North was Mr. Brotherton, a miller who came here from Finley, Ohio, about 1908 and operated the mill a number of years. Mr. Caylor, from Anna, followed Mr. Brotherton and was probably the last miller working there in the 1920's. After the mill ceased manufacturing flour, Monroe Colp, a son of John Colp, had a wholesale grocery on the first floor of a two-story brick building that had been built adjacent on the south side of the mill. The second floor was made into apartments with a long porch with bannisters extending across the entire west front facing South Division. On the east was a near view of the I. C. depot across the tracks below, over which numerous long freight trains rolled by at all hours interspersed with the six daily passenger trains on their regular schedule. Several young married couples felt lucky to get to live in these new apartments until they could buy a home.

After Harve North left the mill he bought the Miles Reed feed and lumber business in a building just south of the mill. The entire business went up in smoke in a spectacular conflagration in 1909 which also burned the First Christian Church close by. This frame church stood on the corner at Brown Street. In the next block was the old First Baptist Church, also frame, with its tall steeple. Dr. J. H. Brooks was the chorister at that church. He had a beautiful baritone voice, and a well-known joke was attributed to him. It has been said by some old-timers that while he was leading his choir in singing one of his favorite hymns, "Will There Be Any Stars in My Crown?" the Christian Church choir would sing, "No, Not One, No, Not One."

Some time after this disastrous fire Harve North joined his brother-in-law, Frank Bracy, in the hardware business in a store next door south of Joe E. Kelley Drug Store. Later Mr. Bracy opened up a store in Herrin and Mr. North had his own hardware establishment across the street in the Washburn building formerly occupied by J. M. Crain, an earlier hardware merchant. Old photographs of both stores show interesting early 20th-century models of gasoline and kerosene cook stoves as well as ornate black heating stoves with nickel plate trimming, having such trade names as "Estate," "Round Oak," "Moore's Hot Blast" and the ultra-modern "Florence" coal burners in three sizes. It is also timely to mention that Bracy-North, later North Hardware, handled the Victor Talking Machines or Victrolas, as is their patented trade name, along with the latest repertoire of up-to-date records, popular, classical and standard music, as well as the comedy variety of that period. These machines all had big horns, brass trimmed; and the more ornate were shaped like a morning glory painted blue with large red roses so attractive to a buyer. These found a ready sale to the numerous coal-mining customers as well as other music lovers. My father purchased one having the "morning glory" horn.

It was on June 27, 1898 that J. W. Russell came to town from Creal Springs, where he had begun the study of photography in 1895 and conducted a successful photograph business there. Reaching Carterville, he opened up his picture studio just across the sidewalk from the old town well with its iron pump and long watering trough nearby. This city well proved a mecca for people far and near, especially for the farmers and their horses to quench their thirsts after a long dusty drive into town from those settlements across Crab Orchard and Grassy Creek.

A colloquialism resulted and is quoted yet today: "If one ever drank once from the old tin cup hanging on the pump, one will always come back to Carterville to reside."

Mr. Russell did lucrative business at this same location until his death in early 1930. Many of the pretty young ladies liked to have their pictures made at Russell's on Sunday afternoon, then go to the nearby depot and board the next incoming passenger train. They, feeling so dressed up in their "Sunday-go-to-meetin' best" with their gorgeously trimmed hats, would ride as far as Crainville, then alight and walk back along the tracks to Carterville. Zella Hayton has stated that this was a regular custom in the early 1900's.

There was another photography shop set up by G. W. Bayless possibly just a few years prior to Mr. Russell's. It came into existence in a most unique way. Its true story has recently been given to me by Mrs. Norma (Dan) Bayless, granddaughter-in-law of Mr. Bayless. When a young man, G. W. owned a thirty-acre farm in the hill country, Grassy and Crab Orchard area, and he wasn't doing well with it. An itinerant salesman, with a camera, called on him one day and demonstrated the camera on a tripod with its blow-gun under its large black cloth covering. Mr. Bayless was so fascinated with this new kind of contraption that the salesman offered to trade it to him for his entire thirty-acre farm. So the bargain was made, and G. W. soon afterwards came to Carterville and opened up his photography studio near the Jeff Cox store. He, also, must have been quite successful in his new venture. Many of our older citizens have examples of his work. I, myself, have a photograph he made of my brother and me, probably in 1897, bearing his photography signature. I with my chubby outstretched baby hands and open mouth was ready to catch the "birdie" when the blow-gun flashed! I presume that after his loss, estimated at $1,000, in the fire of 1898, with only $400 insurance, he never re-established his picture-making business in Carterville.

Jeff Cox had erected his brick building bearing his name and date, 1898, which is still one of the few landmarks in the present business district of Carterville. He, too, had lost heavily due to the big fire. In this new pretentious building he sold furniture and coffins. It is said that after the formal opening of his affluent business he invited his sister-in-law, Mrs. Charles Cash, to view the coffins as well as his fine stock of furniture. The next day, she died. Perhaps, be that as it may, this sad legendary story is worthy of mention to include in Carterville's unique folklore.

The only daughter of Jeff Cox, Jessie, had married Fred Featherstone, who was quite ambitious in promoting his wife's father's prosperous business. So Cox and Featherstone expanded it further on a very large scale, building a huge two-story brick building with a roof garden on top. It was situated farther down the street opposite the town well. The lower floor for modern furniture and pianos—the second floor to be used as an opera house. Carterville had become quite culturally minded. The large roof garden was entirely novel and afforded a beautiful view of the whole business district as well as surrounding residences that could be enjoyed. There was a fine confectionary on top, too, where delicious ice creams and flavored phosphates were served to meet the tastes of the most discriminating who came to the frequent dances for which this "ultra-modern garden" was built.

Not long after its initial opening these enterprising owners engaged a young musician to demonstrate their piano line, by having him sit in the big front plate-glass show-window and play constantly while he was hypnotized. This young man was Arthur Sizemore, only seventeen years old at that time. He lived in Fordville, now known as Energy, three miles east of town, and was known as a "natural-born" musician who could play "any tune by ear." He was a cousin of the noted band conductor, Frank Sizemore. I remember great crowds of people gathered in front of the window to watch him play on and on. I don't know how many hours he played, but it was spectacular advertising. His sister, Mrs. Cora Council, while my guest in 1967, then in her elderly years but possessing a keen memory, related to me how provoked their father was at this publicity stunt. Arthur, when he reached his maturity, went to Chicago and became a composer of music of some renown.

This building also stands out in my memory for the display exhibits of fine needlework and cookery, etc., at Carterville's First Free Fair, set up on a portion of the second floor in beautifully decorated booths under the supervision of Mrs. Emma Elles and Mrs. Zona Watkins. This fine building was short-lived, however, for a fire of unknown origin leveled it to the ground. Thus this is another chapter, so to speak, in the disastrous fires of Carterville's early history.

In 1903, Snyder S. Vick set up a most modern and complete drug store in a quite pretentious new two-story brick building just south of the 1898 Jeff Cox building. For many years the words "S.S. Vick Drug Store," painted in large yellow letters, could be seen on the south wall high up on its second story. This upper part housed his father's, Dr. J. W. Vick's, medical office, and also that of another prominent physician and surgeon, Dr. B. F. Crain. Some years later after Dr. Crain became resident physician at the newly established Holden Hospital, Carbondale, his office was occupied by Dr. F. M. Hiller.

On the same floor was also the law office of Judge J. L. Gallimore, which faced Division Street. Judge Gallimore in 1893 had come to Carterville from Golconda as a young attorney and rose to become a prominent County Judge of Williamson County, holding this office for many years. Dr. John W. Vick had begun his practice in Carterville in 1882, and is accredited with planting shade trees, especially maples, along Division Street, which to this day make this long thoroughfare from north to south a spectacular stretch of scenic beauty at each autumn's coloring.

Dr. Vick was president of the school board and the board of health for twenty years. He maintained his medical practice

43

here for fifty years. It is not surprising that his two sons, Snyder and Jay, being reared in a doctor's home, would be ambitious to become druggists. Accordingly both were educated in pharmacy at Northwestern University. Jay had just finished his pharmaceutical training in 1918, and in August of that year Snyder sold a half-interest in his store to Jay. Snyder moved to Johnston City, where he had purchased a drug store in that rapidly growing mining town. Under Jay's efficient management the Carterville store had an unexcelled prescription department and sold fine candies, high-grade pipes and cigars, and popular brands of cosmetics. Columbia graphaphones and records were also handled, as well as Eastman Kodaks and films. The beautiful up-to-date soda fountain and the latest magazines and daily newspapers of that day soon popularized it to be a favorite shopping place. The late Sara Spiller, Reba Carter and Dorothy Stocks Phillips and Beulah Griggs were capable clerks there for many years. This store had the distinction of being one of the three "mother" stores of Carterville that established other branches in Southern Illinois.

Many interesting stories can be told centered around this drug store. One particular happening I definitely remember was in the days of the Birger-Shelton gang era in the 1920's. One Saturday night in the early part of the evening a group of us Carterville young schoolteachers had stopped at "Vick's" to be served and sip the popular "cherry cokes" that only the inimitable Reba Carter could so delectably blend. As we sat at one of the ice-cream tables in the center of the store, a nicely dressed and very handsome young man in a gray suit entered, stopped at the front counter, purchased some cigars and walked casually out. We learned later he was Art Newman, a member of that notorious criminal gang that was harassing all Southern Illinois. Although he had already come and gone, we literally quaked in our shoes.

Some stories concerning Dr. Vick and Dr. Crain, both of whom were early "horse and buggy" doctors, that bear repeating have been related to me by Mrs. John Hutton, nee Vera

44

Sizemore. She was a trained nurse and often was called upon by one or the other to go on an emergency or difficult case. She vividly remembers Dr. Crain telling her on one such occasion this true story, which I herewith quote: Dr. Vick asked Dr. Crain to go out with him in Dr. Vick's buggy to a place in the country over a bumpy road full of chug-holes. Finally Dr. Vick said, "Dr. Crain, you take the reins, and I'm going back and see what that d—d noise is." Dr. Vick got out and walked back a distance, then hollered to Dr. Crain: "Hold him Doc!" Coming back to the buggy he took the reins, never said a word until Dr. Crain remarked to him, "Did you find the trouble, Doc?" "Yes, it's not a dangerous situation but it's d—d nerve wracking." What the trouble was, the buggy springs were weak and its bed would hit the frame every time they struck a chug-hole. Vera has said she can still hear Dr. Crain laughing as he told this tale on Dr. Vick to her. Another humorous incident she remembers about them: Again these two doctors were riding together over a very muddy road south of town. All at once the buggy hit a deep mud-hole in the black gumbo, sinking one of the wheels to the axle, and Dr. Vick said to Dr. Crain, "Here, take the reins," and immediately hopped out of the buggy to investigate. As he got back into the buggy again Dr. Crain asked him, "Did we break a spring?" To which Dr. Vick replied, "No, but it is mighty inconvenient"—as he whipped up the horse to pull them out of this dilemma!

Dr. Vick's faithful buggy horse was named "Dan." Lena Beasley Martin's father, Elmer Beasley, had a blacksmith shop on Walnut Street just a short distance back of the Vick Building, and the doctor regularly left his horse hitched in the buggy shed adjoining Mr. Beasley's shop at the rear. Many times Lena recalls he would telephone the Beasley residence, which was just across the driveway from the "smithy," and say to Mrs. Beasley, "Becky, go over and tell Elmer to make Old Dan quit pawing the wall!" The doctor was a keen observer and listener from the rear windows in his office, and apparently his noisesome steed, grown nervous while standing

45

hitched, had exasperated the good doctor's patience as well as disturbing his office routine. Since Dr. Vick had located in Carterville approximately eleven years after the village began, the following story personifies the great demand and impressive popularity he sought to build up a growing lucrative practice. As someone has said, he often drove very fast on the long stretch of Division Street, indicating there was an urgency to answer speedily the apparently many calls in the need for his services.

There is more to be told about Beasley's Smithy, which displayed at its very top a huge sign painted in box-car letters: E. BEASLEY, BLACKSMITH—BUGGIES-CARRIAGES-WAGONS.

Horse-shoeing was a thriving business there; and in addition, as was common then, blacksmiths manufactured nails, scythes, harness fastenings, plowshares and sometimes even swords as well as pots and pans.

David C. Bogard, father of alderman John Bogard, on coming to Carterville from Kentucky, at Mr. Beasley's request, began his work in this smithy about 1906. He designed and forged an iron emblem on a perpendicular rod with the insignia "M. W. of A." at the top of it—this to be used to mark the grave of a deceased Woodman brother in our Oakwood Cemetery on Memorial (Decoration) Day. This was made at the suggestion of Dr. A. J. Aird who was a member of that fraternal organization. John Bogard has a treasured photo of his father and Dr. Aird sitting side by side holding this unique marker between them.

Dr. Aird had come to Carterville soon after the turn of the century from Olive Branch, and hung out his shingle for general practice. He served this community as a physician and surgeon many years until his death some time after 1945. He purchased the old Carver property in the 200 block of North Division Street just the other side of Holmes Garage, remodeling and transforming it into a residence of unusual beauty with its many criss-crossed, paned casement windows and a beautiful front sun parlor. It later burned, but his separate office nearby directly facing the street was saved and continued to be used throughout his long practice. Alberta Crain Throgmorton was his dependable office girl a number of years. It was his custom to walk when making calls on his patients in town, at which times he issued his prescribed pills, capsules, powders or liquids from his medical satchels.

The large red-brick edifice built by the Modern Woodmen, of which Dr. Aird was so proud, is located at the corner of East Illinois and Walnut Streets just a short distance north of Beasley's Blacksmith Shop. On its facade in white-brick trim is the following: "MW of A., 1899 6234 1910," which authenticates this structure. The upper story contained three rooms. The largest, fronting East Illinois Street, was the lodge hall for both the Modern Woodmen of America and its sister fraternal order, the Royal Neighbors of America. It was used from 1914 through 1921 for the Alumni receptions of the Carterville High School; and even after 1915 a number of yearly Junior-Senior banquets were given there, all of which were put on in great style.

In the southwest part of the upper floor was another large room, big enough to accomodate ninety-five school desks for as many fifth-grade pupils and a pot bellied stove plus teacher's desks for the two teachers, Ruth Lauder (Volner) and myself, who taught those children the 1918-1919 school term. The third smaller room across the hall on the southeast side was the "paddling room," if such became necessary, as it frequently did. The limited playground was the small vacant lot behind Vick's Drug Store. No doubt this contributed to the discipline problems with which we had to deal.

The Carterville Grade Schools were overflowing at that time. This was the period of World War I, when the coal mining industry of this area had attracted labor from everywhere. The mines, railroads and commercial institutions were going at top speed and had been for months preceding our country's declaration of war against Germany. So the schools naturally were overpopulated. The three existing school buildings could not contain all the grade children and the high-school students, too.

At the north side were two school buildings, the old two-story, four-room frame with its long porch across its back entrance, and the two-and-one-half-story brick building that had been built in 1899. From its window belfry its huge bell rang out every morning and noontime, also at both recesses, calling the boys and girls to classes. This bell had a beautiful tone, and what a pleasing clarion it was, especially on the first day of school each fall! There were two wells covered with small latticed houses—one between the frame and the brick; the other stood at the southwest corner of the latter. In my early childhood the school children quenched their thirsts from water buckets with tin cups there, and sometimes the teachers would allow those to be passed up and down the aisles after a very warm afternoon at play. Toilet accommodations were outside privies, which word was then considered crude and most uncouth. Mrs. Kate Dowell, a beloved first-grade teacher for many years, used to tell a cute story about how she was trying to impress a little girl to say "Toilet" when necessary to leave the room; but it was to no avail when the little girl said, "I've always said privy and I'm still going to say privy." So there were little rebels then!

I wonder how many remember the "banner ditch" that bordered the school yard a short distance from the front south entrance of the old frame along Anderson Street? A favorite spot, too, in playing "follow the leader" for small children. No fancy playground equipment then. This revered building was torn down in the early 1920's and the old brick was demolished by bulldozers in August, 1969. Many present-day citizens were saddened even though it was for progress.

During the school terms of 1916-1917 and 1917-1918 a new frame bungalow-type building erected by the First Baptist Church as a Sunday School annex on South Division very near the south wall of the church was rented by the School Board. The fifth grade was taught in 1916-1917 by Roxana Snyder and Edna Bevard, and the following term 1917-1918

Zoe McNeill (Sizemore) and Lelia Caplinger (Hayton) taught the seventh grade there.

Just before Christmas 1919 the new Park School building was finished. I was one of the lucky teachers to be assigned there. The two fifth grades had split time from September to December that fall, holding school a half-day each in the rented Sunday School room of the Christian Church. I shall always remember the kindness of J. B. Samuel to me in loaning me his old hand bell that he had used when a rural teacher, before he started his lumber business when Carterville was very young. I have many memories of my teaching years in the Park Building; and each springtime when I see the delicate pink blossoms on the beautiful large apricot tree in Mrs. Leona Gregory's back yard, which is close to this building, it recalls to my mind the many years she served chili and hamburgers for the school children before the days of federally aided lunch rooms. One incident stands out. I had gone over to Lena Beasley's third-grade room in the old brick one noontime. It was drizzling rain that warm spring day, and she had sent Billy Carol Carter to Mrs. Gregory's to get a bowl of chili for her. The windows on the east, next to the sidewalk, were up. Shortly we heard voices. It was Billy Carol and his chum Joe Adams, and Joe was prevailing on Billy Carol to hurry, when Billy replied: "I can't. Do you want me to spill the old lady's soup?"

Now, taking up my story thread and connecting it to East Illinois Avenue, I must mention the historic two-story red brick with dove-tailed, buff-colored stone trim that was built by the Illinois Engineering Company at the Hickory Street Corner, in reality a continuation of Walnut Street. The stockholders were Fred Richart and the Zimmerman brothers. It was sold some time after it was built to the CIPS Company and was commonly known as the Electric Light Building. It is now owned by Jones Electric. I feel a certain nostalgia yet, everytime I go to pay my current electric bill collected by Cleo Jones there; for one of my happiest school years was spent in its upper north room as a seventh-grader with Julian

Illinois Engineering Company

This building was sold to be used as Carterville City Hall; in 1969 it became the Public Library. L to r.: George Presley, Henry Skelcher; Al Arterberry; Ben Thaxton; Ed Gallagher; George Beltz, on team; Guy Caplinger; Herbert W. Cann, Mayor. The little girl, far left, is Rhea Harris, now Mrs. Roy O'Neill of Hurst. She thinks the picture was made before 1910. The house was formerly the McNeill Hotel, first in the village.

Atwood as our teacher. This was 1908-1909, when there was not adequate room for all the elementary grades in the two north-side school buildings, and this inadequacy necessitated the erection of the South Side School, which became a reality at the corner of Pennsylvania and Blossom Streets about 1910 or 1911. There was an outside iron stairway, a fire escape, on the east side of the "Light" building leading up to our seventh-grade room, which we tramped up and down daily instead of the interior wooden steps between the downstairs offices.

The South Side School building existed about forty years and met the fate of being torn down, as had the North Side Schools. However, during the early part of the Depression, so many families had moved from Carterville seeking employment in industrial cities and elsewhere, the town's population had decreased greatly. Ten grade-school teachers in the system in 1930 became among the unemployed. The Illinois Emergency Relief Commission with its staff of caseworkers for this area centered its work in the vacated old South Side.

Barbershop in Rear of J. V. Walker Store
Barbers: Tommy Council; Malcolm Sims; George Watkins; customers:
John McNeill, Rev. R. O. Rogers; Dr. J. W. Wick. Inset above: George
Watkins, Malcolm Sims, Harvey Crain.

A Baptism at Mill Pond, Crainville; at left, Rev. J. W. McKinney baptizes
John Spires, a Carterville area school teacher.

Carterville Flour Mill, built in 1894

CHAPTER II

MORE METAMORPHOSIS

Some time ago I mentioned the three-chair barber shop inside the J. V. Walker building, and just outside its south entrance the barber pole advertising "BATHS." Just recently I have been informed by Oscar Jones, owner of Jones Electric, that there is still a large tank on the upper floor of his building that was used to store water, piped up from a deep well on the east outside; and another pipe further extended to this barber shop, there being no city waterworks here. This, to me, solves the quandary of wonderment about this unusual service provided for the shop's fastidious patrons in those days.

Another story relating to that particular shop has just been told to me by Lelia (Caplinger) Hayton, stepdaughter of M. W. Sizemore, the first cashier of the Carterville State and Savings Bank. The Sizemore family, about the time the "Light" building was erected, resided in a yellow frame two-story dwelling right across the street, south, which is now the location of the Masonic Temple at Walnut and East Illinois. Lelia remembers one Easter season when she was about eight years old that she was all dressed up in her new wool challis frock her mother had made, feeling, oh, so proud! Passing this barber shop, someone suddenly opened the door and expectorated a great gob of tobacco juice which spattered her frock all over. Whoever it was had apparently failed to notice the one convenient spittoon which the shop afforded and didn't anticipate a passer-by. Her dress was thoroughly ruined —no known methods, either, of removing the ugly brownish stains.

The Masonic Temple was not erected until 1927, but it

played a most significant role in the affairs of this community. Its dedication by Governor Louis L. Emmerson of Illinois drew a great crowd of Masons and Eastern Stars with their invited guests. Mrs. Zella (Sizemore) Scott, daughter of the bank cashier, was Worthy Matron and presided most graciously. This occasion was really a highlight for both father and daughter, and the whole town was elated to have been honored by a Governor's visit—the first of record here.

The Temple had a fairly large stage downstairs with adjoining dressing rooms which were appropriate for grade school operettas to be given, as well as school plays. On one occasion I remember our High School Alumni put on a three-act play. I believe it was titled, *The Dear Boy Graduates*. The players were graduates prior to 1930 and were happy to enact it for the benefit of the school. Miss Agnes Stewart, teacher in the eighth grade here many years, had a leading part. In the third act she was to use a toy pistol to represent a "Gatlin'" gun, but somehow in the excitement off stage it became lost and she grabbed at the crucial moment a pair of scissors and rushed out of the dressing room just in the nick of time to speak the closing lines and "shoot" (with scissors pointed) as Evan Phillips, the hero, innovated a "boom-boom" sound to the amusement of all. The toy pistol was never found, however, and remains a mystery to this day.

Many children who performed in the yearly grade-school operettas directed either by the music teachers Lucille (Hadfield) Lamar or Tressie (Visconti) Senese, with piano accompanists, Hessie Carter (Gall) and Alvera Bazetta, usually in the early spring, perhaps now, even though parents or grandparents they can recall the happiness they experienced at these benefit performances for our beloved school. Grades one through eight participated, and all the elementary teachers cooperated in making the stage scenery, also the lavish decorations and sometimes even the costumes for the underprivileged children—extra-curricular activities most times at night without pay. In 1930 the school board took action to not hire a regular music teacher on the faculty, so this curtailed operettas. Not until the early 1940's when Miss Irene Watson was employed to be music instructor for both the grade school and the Carterville Community High School were these musical entertainments revived. An outstanding grade school operetta she directed was "Tom Sawyer," which was given on the CCHS stage, since by that time the stage in the Temple had been removed and a modern kitchen installed in its place.

I wonder how many living today remember the big flood of 1937 when the Ohio River and its Southern Illinois tributaries went on a terrible rampage, bringing much distress to the Cairo and Paducah areas? There were ninety or more colored "refugees" from Mound City that were brought to Carterville to receive emergency care until the Red Cross could rehabilitate them. Hot vegetable soup prepared by the Woman's Club and other local women, bread, milk and coffee provided by the grocery stores were served to them in the Temple, as many teachers aided. The citizenry of the town assembled blankets, quilts and clothing for them to be bedded there. Much could be written about the sad plight of those men, women, and children whose homes had been swept away. These unfortunate people were lodged here a week or more, but left with a deep and, humble gratitude in their hearts for the compassion shown to them, which was indeed an example of Christianity in action! Frank Ledbetter, editor of the *Carterville Herald* at that time, also owned and edited *The Pulaski Enterprise,* a popular newspaper in Mound City. His business there was completely ruined.

The J. J. Hunter building adjoining the M. W. of A. edifice was built in 1902, as its white-brick trims show. Mr. Hunter was a prominent furniture dealer as well as an undertaker. In those days there were no funeral homes here—more commonly designated as "funeral parlors." A booklet titled "Old Time Songs" (price 10c) purchased from him by my father, who had bought several items of his "fashionable" furniture, shows on the back cover pictures of both the outer and interior views of his building. Below these his ad reads as follows:

LICENSED   EMBALMER   LICENSED

DEALER IN
FASHIONALE
FURNITURE
ORGANS, SEWING MACHINES
UNDERTAKING
YOURS TRULY,
J. J. HUNTER

Mr. Hunter is pictured in the foreground of the interior standing near an upright piano, and nearby are a child's rocking chair and two little wagons. Before he retired a few years later, Henry Riggin worked for him as an embalmer beginning in 1907. Some time afterwards Mr. Riggin operated an undertaking establishment for Albert Storme in Herrin. The late Frank Hill after Hunter's retirement became sole manager of the store and served as undertaker. Not long afterwards Mr. Hill and his father bought the entire stock, incorporating it under the name of W. E. Hill and Son Furniture Store. They later moved this business to a building on South Division on the spot where the Josh Walker Livery Stable had stood. The building was enlarged and in 1925 Fred Hoover joined the Hill firm. A humorous incident occurred about 1923 when Grace Walker, one of the South Side School teachers, and I had gone into the store to look at the new furniture there. Grace was particularly interested in shopping for a mattress and Mr. Hill was showing her a well-known brand explaining the fine workmanship, quality, etc., when suddenly she asked, "Are any of these guaranteed not to sag?" And all of us unconsciously and modestly blushed!

In 1922 Charles Simpson opened up his Ford Agency and garage in the building formerly occupied by Harve North's Hardware on South Division. Then was the period of prosperous automobile sales after World War I. Cecil Baker (Etherton), daughter of John Baker, who had a dry goods store where Pulley's T. V. Shop is now, was the popular bookkeeper for the Simpson Motor Sales. The Frost Furniture Store now occupies the entire space that Simpson and Hill formerly owned, including the popular W. V. Craig Grocery Store location adjoining.

Mr. Simpson and a young mechanic, Johnny Spiller, were aviation enthusiasts. Gilbert D. Wallace, a Carterville native residing now in Huron, Ohio, has sent me the following story, and I quote: "For years I tended cows for neighbors. The mines near Carterville leased me their lake and meadows, and I drove cattle there to graze in the morning, and after school drove them back to be milked. At that time many, many people kept cows in town and there was no ordinance against it. Among my customers were Lockies, Ben Perry, the Huttons, and Mr. L. G. Crain, who was on the board of education. The pasture was divided into two sections, both which allowed use of the mine lake or pond. Aviation was a novelty then. It was Mr. Spiller's hopes to be able to share whichever pasture was free at the time for landing his plane, as it would save him miles of travel.

"We hit a bargain. For the privilege, I was to be given instructions in flying, free flights occasionally on week-ends, etc. It never worked out that way. I read up all I could on flying, but as months wore on Mr. Spiller could never find the time for me though my fields were in constant use. One Saturday I had been put off long enough. I climbed aboard the plane after unhooking the guy wires that anchored it. A friend (I believe it was Willard Webber) cranked the plane by turning the prop. On ignition it started and then the wooden wheel blocks were removed and, hopping across the field, I somehow became airborne, but made the fatal mistake of flying too low over Carterville. Spiller recognized his plane and was fighting mad when Oscar Bloodworth (taxi-man) rushed him to the flight field and I finally brought it down in a series of bounces. It was for me a terrifying flight, and the tongue-lashing I received lasted me for years to come. It was almost fifteen years before my interest again returned to flying. This time I took the necessary training and received my license in proper order. Mr. Spiller would not stand the risk of trusting me again and the same day removed his plane from the field and never again returned to the pond pasture."

Getting back to Frank Hill. Mr. Hill saw the need of a nice funeral home for this town. He had purchased the attractive and practically new Carlisle house (one-story) where Blossom Street intersects South Division. A novel engineering feat began. The entire roof was lifted and a second story built under it to be used as living quarters while the lower first floor was outfitted into a lovely commodious funeral home, which was probably the first of its kind in Carterville.

In the meanwhile Henry Riggin came back to Carterville to resume his embalming work in the Hampton Building where Dr. Fine's office is now, but soon afterwards moved across the street where Heckel's hardware is located. He remained there until 1930 when he went into business for himself in the 300 block of North Division, where his son Gordon, whom he trained in the business, now has a very beautiful and impressive colonial-style mortuary.

Now, again I pick up a dangling thread of thought to tell about the post office on East Illinois Avenue that occupied the lower floor of the two-story brick owned by Roy Norton, son of Mrs. Axie Norton, manager of the famed Carterville Hotel and the no-less-noted Norton House (the former Dr. Brooks' fabulous home). The post office faced the J. J. Hunter building; however, it had been moved there from a former location in the Hampton building. Some time in the 1950's it met a disastrous fate by fire. It was moved as soon as possible to the American Legion building next to Holmes Garage. During the Kennedy Administration a modern new post office building was erected on the triangular lot between the Illinois Central main track and East Grand Avenue. The old Illinois Central Railroad depot had been torn down there after many years of useful service to passengers and a heavy trade in handling express and freight in Carterville's heyday.

The upper story above the old Post Office on East Illinois housed a very important communication medium. It was the telephone exchange known as "Central," with its old-fashioned switchboard and a separate business office. There were many "telephone girls," most generally personated as "hello-girls," employed there who worked on day and night shifts. And there was a "Chief Operator." Which recalls to my mind the first telephone my father had installed in our house—the date, about 1905, I think. Oh, how wondreful it was—a long-boxed wall affair with two bells at the top and batteries inside the box, also a crank to ring "central" and request certain numbers wanted! These types of phones now are collector's items on the antique market. I recall further a popular song composed in that era. The chorus words of it were these:

> "Hello, Central, give me heaven,
> For my mama's there.
> You will find her with the angels
> on the golden stair."

My mother liked to hear me sing it, especially when we had company! But its plaintive sadness, although a sweet tune, still haunts my memory. Some of the "hello-girls" were Anna Templeton, Kate Crain (Buckley), Hattie Ardery, Hazel Jordan and the chief operator, Mae Volner, and later Hope Hadfield. Mrs. Dora Royster worked in the office.

The Woman's Club cabin, east of the Masonic Temple, should not be overlooked in this metamorphosis story. The club was organized in 1915 and Miss Minnie Ferrell was the first president. She was the daughter of the noted Dr. H. V. Ferrell, one of the two earliest doctors in this area. A Doctor Fain, the other one, served this community in the 1870's. The cabin was built by WPA labor in the early 1930's (Depression years). The club had held its regular meetings in the homes of members until the cabin clubroom was provided. The cabin is truly symbolic of our early American heritage; and although it is rustic on the outside it is now beautifully modern inside, which indicates the progressive spirit of its loyal members. When it was built the laborers used native yellow-birch sapling poles on walls and ceiling inside, but in time this type of

57

timber proved impractical and the walls are panelled now. It was while Miss Ferrell was president that the Carterville Woman's Club started the first library here about 1916, and it was housed in the back room of the old Carterville State and Savings Bank. But after a few years it ceased to be, and the bank rented the room to the Carterville Building and Loan Association. There was an outside entrance on West Illinois Avenue. Older residents recall that office did a huge volume of business in Carterville's very prosperous days from 1910 to 1930. When the bank was remodelled the entrance was bricked up as were the windows.

Another outstanding community service this club originated and still maintains is the Carterville Woman's Club Cemetery Fund for the upkeep of Oakwood and Hillcrest Cemeteries. In reference to Oakwood, George M. McNeill, co-founder of Carterville, sold ten acres off his farm to the city for a mere pittance (his daughter, Merta Sonner, affirms in her recent letter to me). The land was from his "home place" which he bought in 1878; and the family moved there at the dead end of Dobson Street from the hotel about 1883, when Merta was five years old. Merta further states in the letter, "I remember when he came home from the board meeting he told my mother about it and she almost got a divorce from him as she didn't want that cemetery there. Frank Bevard bought the first lot before they had the lots laid off (for burial of his small child). The grave was made in the street and it had to be moved." One of the original virgin oaks still stands near the Bevard lot.

It is interesting to know that the purchase price at first was $5.00 per lot; but the prices steadily increased to ten, fifteen, twenty-five, fifty dollars, until today the cost is two hundred dollars.

There is quite a history connected with the Carterville State and Savings Bank that stands at the corner of South Division and West Illinois. It was on April 12, 1904 that the stock-holders of the private Bank of Carterville, who were Charles H. Dennison and John H. Burnett of Marion and Sam H.

Bundy of Carterville, decided to incorporate; and the Carterville State and Savings Bank was formed, with M. W. Sizemore as the first cashier, S. H. Bundy first president, and J. B. Samuel, vice president. In its long history it has had only six presidents. M. W. Sizemore continued as cashier until the bank was closed on April 12, 1930 during the Depression. It is significant to note that all seven banks in Williamson County were closed on that same date. The First National Bank of Carterville had occupied the opposite South Division corner site and had also been a prosperous banking institution. That fatal blow to our town, I well remember. The First National was never reopened. The new office of the Carterville Water and Sewer department occupies the building at present. It already having the original bank vault adds to this office's convenience.

The first location of the Carterville State and Savings Bank was two doors south of Vick's Drug Store. After the bank was moved to its new building on the corner, its former space contained Lizzie Crain's Millinery Store about 1915. Other milliners who worked for her were her neice Ruth Porritt (Tuberville) and Mae and Pearl Deason, also Belle Winning; and the beautiful creations of their hats were works of art. The millinery trade was a prosperous business here at that time.

Leo Watson went to work in the bank on May 24, 1908 and was made assistant cashier to his uncle, M. W. Sizemore, on January 10, 1910. When the bank reopened on April 12, 1931 he became cashier and served in that capacity until February 16, 1952, when the bank was sold to other stockholders. He had the distinction of serving fifty years as a banker in his hometown bank before his retirement—the bank that is known far and wide as "Williamson County's Oldest Bank."

Although during the Depression it was closed from April 12, 1930 to April 12, 1931, it is proud of the fact that every depositor of the bank when it was closed received one hundred cents for each dollar on deposit. It was the first bank out of seven in Williamson County to reopen its doors. Oren Coleman and Walter Rowatt saw distinguished service in the office of president after its reopening.

The bank, now having been completely remodeled, is one of the most modern in Southern Illinois and has the most modern banking equipment obtainable. Its new red brick building with white columns that resembles a beautiful Grecian temple, at the corner of East Grand Avenue and South Division, is ultra-modern as a drive-up convenience. This site was formerly that of the old Carterville Hotel that originally was ·named the "Alexander," built in 1910. Thus that portion of the "cocoon" of old Carterville at this particular site by the main Illinois Central Railroad track has burst into full glory—so beautifully landscaped, too, with evergreens and bright red tulips for spring, and multi-colored petunias in the summer. The building, graced by its tall neon sign giving time and temperature each minute, will be a landmark at this prominent focal point of the business district for years to come. It should be considered a memorial to the leadership of our noted former bankers, as well as to the aggressiveness of the present bank officers, Oscar Schafale, president, and Lloyd C. Henderson, executive vice president. The directors are Jettie Vaughn, Gordon Riggin, Matt Steffes, Jo V. Walker, Donald D. Gentry and Phil Heckel, with Oscar Schafale, chairman of the board.

Business places in the short block of East Illinois Avenue would not be complete without mentioning the small building just around the corner off South Division that now houses the McGraw News Agency. It was the place where the genial and enterprising businessman R. H. H. Hampton had set up his insurance business after he went broke operating his first drug store in 1876. By 1906 he was well on his way financially and had built the large two-story Hampton Building on North Division, moving his entire business there. The Hampton Drug Company remained under the family management until his daugther, Ruth (Hampton) Washburn, sold it to Larry Brymer about two years ago. His widow Margaret and her sister, Miss Tena Thompson, with Mrs. Maud (Chat) Hampton and Mrs. Washburn, carried it on for many years. Maud Beadles, who became the wife of Mr. Hampton's only son Chat (now deceased), came to Carterville from Quincy in the second decade of this century to handle the bookkeeping and insurance business. To her many friends she was known as "Bea." She succeeded Ted Hill of Freeburg, Illinois as bookkeeper for the firm. He had begun his work at Hamptons around 1908. Mr. Hill and Leo Watson had met while students at "G.M.C."—Gem City Business College in Quincy, Illinois—and Leo had recommended Ted for the job, telling him that Carterville, a promising town, would be a good place to work, as he himself had obtained a position as assistant cashier in the Carterville State and Savings Bank.

The Hampton Building housed the post office about that time when James A. Lauder was postmaster, and his successor, L. E. Robertson, who is best known as the first editor of the *Carterville Herald* and who began its publishing on August 24, 1899.

The small Hampton Insurance office building has had several tenants prior to the present news agency, which succeeded a similar agency operated in the 1950's by Reuben and Opal Jent. However, during the Depression years Mrs. Reba Ridley carried on a popular "beauty shop" business there for several years, later moving over the Carterville State and Savings Bank in the former dental office of Dr. Frank Washburn.

It is significant at this point to insert in this story some pertinent information from Mrs. Janice Lockie Searl, granddaughter of Doctor W. H. Perry, who operated his own drug store at the corner of South Division and Illinois Avenue in 1883 and 1884. Some microfilm copies from her grandfather's store ledger verifies his account for sundry items purchased from Collins Brothers, wholesale druggists, St. Louis, Missouri, December 12, 1883, in the amount of $58.45 and paid December 20, 1983. A facsimile microfilm copy of a statement to one of the doctor's patients is as follows:

```
                        M. Jas McEwan
                        in account with
                        W. H. Perry M.D.
          1883
          Oct. 2      To ext tooth self                    .50
          1884
          Feb. 5         ”   visit                        1.00
              5         ”   Amico 35 & Arnica 35           .70
              7         ”   Arnica 35 & Arnica 35          .70
                                                         _____
                                                          2.90
```

Apparently Dr. Perry also was a dentist.
Janice adds this note:

"I think Grandpa went to take more medical courses in
Chicago at Rush Medical School about 1884. He first practiced with Dr. H. V. Ferrell in a log cabin situated on the
farm now owned by Ted and Gethel Hill east of Carterville.
Later he opened an office where the Tiny Tot Shop is now
located."

When I was six or seven years old I had the measles and
chicken-pox. I remember Dr. Perry calling to see me and
opening up his satchel to issue powders which he folded inside
little papers. He had walked from his office.

Another microfilm Janice has included pertains to a pro-
gramme given by the Young People's Literary Society in the
High School Room, Friday Evening, February 4, 1910, beginning at 7:30 o'clock, as follows:

> Address of Welcome—J. W. McKinney
> Instrumental Solo—Ruth Hampton
> Recitation—Zora Brandon
> Recitation—Joy Wright
> Current Events—Ben Perry
> Vocal Duet— Inez and Oda Hiller
> Humorous Reading—Ethel Jordan
> Recitation—Laura Crain
> Recitation—Bonnie Kunz
> Essay—Minnie Bracy
> Recitation—Margarite Hoffman
> Vocal Duet—Maud Whitacre and Emma Walker

Some who read this may recall that J. W. McKinney after leaving the school was elected Williamson County Superintendent of Schools, with office in Marion, and moved to our county seat where he served several terms.

There is more to be said about the M.W. of A. building and the business places facing the Beasley Blacksmith shop, and thence around the alley leading just a short distance back to South Division—circling the block, so to speak.

The Chevrolet Motor Sales, managed by Mr. and Mrs. Will Allen in the early 1920's, did a flourishing business. Later Brown & Colombo had a large grocery there, succeeded afterward by one owned by Harold Walker. Today the Tregoning "House of Antiques" contains a wealth of old treasures in that vast floor space which has been a mecca for yearly auction sales that attract buyers and dealers from far and near.

Just behind the House of Antiques a smaller brick and block building stood for many years facing the Beasley Shop. James Cagle had a small grocery and cream station there in the early 1920's. Carlista Jones, now a well-known cosmetologist here, has given me a delightful story that was her experience as a grade-school child when she went to her Uncle Jim Cagle's store and asked for fifty cents' worth of onions. He forthwith sacked up about a half-bushel, and she went trudging out with the bulky load. Happily, before she got very far she met her father and he helped her take it back. Her error in misjudging the current price of onions was a standing joke with Mr. Cagle and Papa Jones for a long, long time. In due time the Cagle store went out of business and was superseded by Jim Bledsoe's Cleaning and Pressing Shop for a while after World War II. In the meantime Otis Ragland had set up his own cream station and feed store in the front of the old blacksmith shop.

Earl Brookshire was managing Melvin Hall's frozen food locker in the 1940's directly behind Mel's Supermarket; and to reach this market, which ocupied the large building formerly owned by Baker-Ghent General Merchandise Store facing South Division, one could enter through the Walnut Street side, walk past the locker direct into the grocery department and come out on the Division Street front. After Ramsey Hall and Gene Stocks became owners of this historic building it was torn down, and their Food Land prefabricated building was erected flush with Walnut Street. The space formerly graced by the old store was converted to a black-topped parking lot which is now used for Bay's Food-Land customers.

It is said that a Chinese laundry was located for a while near this location, facing Walnut Street, prior to 1900; but I've never learned the name of the laundryman, nor do I know his method of washing—suffice it to say it must have been in the obsolete rub-a-dub manner by washboard and tub. But it is of timely interest to know that, after a period of perhaps three quarters of a century, a modern laundromat equipped with electric automatic washers and dryers was installed by Wade Rowatt almost directly across from the Chinaman's laundry on the west side of South Division. I might term this in a way in the turn of events as a coincidental consequence.

Before Hall and Stocks set up their "Food-Land" they purchased the store building and stock that had been used by Leon Bevard for his independent grocery and meat market for many years. It was situated between the Baker-Ghent building and the original Carterville State and Savings Bank location. The popular Leo Birkholz grocery and meat market for many years occupied the old bank building as successor to a similar grocery and market operated at an earlier time by Robert Maaska on the same spot.

While mentioning independent grocery stores that flourished a number of years on South Division Street, there were those of Arch Howell, Leo Scott, W. V. Craig, and the firm of

64

Hayton and West, the latter located between the old Bonita Theatre and the Carterville Hotel. The late Gladys Smith worked one summer at Hayton and West's. I remember an incident she related to me. A certain regular customer bought kerosene for her lamps and oil cook stove. Each time she would follow Gladys into the back room to watch as Gladys turned the spigot on at the big tank, and each time would request that Gladys not place the half-potato back on the spigot until the last drop had dripped into the customer's gallon oil can, which exasperated Gladys no little bit. But the lady was bound to get her money's worth. W. V. Craig came here from Tennessee to work as a clerk in the growing business of Moake and Impson General Merchandise Store. Sometime later he bought one of the smaller grocery stores and became a very successful merchant here for many years.

T. J. Moake and his brother-in-law, Frank Impson, in the very early days of Carterville established the Moake and Impson General Merchandise Store. It catered to the farmers' trade and had its own hitchrack back of the store and stepping stones in the front to accommodate the lady customers, especially as they alighted from the buggies or wagons. Mr. Moake was one of the first bank directors of the Carterville State and Saving Bank. The store was affluent for many years. Hooker's Department Store is situated now in the former Moake and Impson establishment.

Imagine if you will a tall, dark, red-painted, four-room, two-story building in an "L" shape, two large rooms to the west and two to the north with a broad hallway in between, and the stairway boarded up to the second floor. This was the old schoolhouse where Miss Kate Winning and Miss Lily Hope taught under the superintendency of James M. Turner. It was Mr. Turner who founded the Crab Orchard Academy in 1889 and had organized the Carterville High School in 1899. This four-room school stood a short distance west off South Division Street but faced south on West Grand Avenue. In those days it was a prominent corner and still is—the present location of the Don Gentry Insurance Agency. Roxy Snyder has told me her vivid recollections regarding this school. Underneath the blackboard in the primary room was an elevated platform all along the floor for the children to stand on when sent to the "board" to do their numbers, in order that they could reach it comfortably. When in the third grade, she and her classmates and the other children marched hand in hand over to the white frame school and the new red brick one, just completed in 1899, on the north side of town in the edge of the "grove." The first three grades were settled in the white building—the fourth grade got to go in the new brick one. Florence Hill taught third grade and had the distinction of going on with this class as they advanced through the eighth grade. She was a daughter of Warren Hill, teacher of pioneer fame in this area.

You may ask what happened to the building vacated. Two rooms of it were converted into a dwelling and moved over a short distance to the corner of Oak Street and West Grand, which is the present location of the Grand Avenue Baptist Church. This dwelling was a residence later of Mrs. Alice Watson Payne and her daughter, Hazel Watson, for some years. Hazel is now Mrs. Mark Phemister. Mrs. Payne was an expert seamtress: I remember the fittings for my eighth grade graduation dress when she was residing there in 1910. The rest of the building was torn down and on that lot was built a lovely large brick residence by William Stevenson—called "English Bill," a coal miner who had brought his family here from England soon after the turn of the century. Later it was purchased by John Colp of Carterville Milling and Coal operation fame. At present this massive impressive dwelling, reminiscent of London substantial homes, is the parsonage of the church next door.

There was a small cottage in the middle of the corner lot, between the red school building and South Division, which was skirted by the railroad tracks (two at that time). Dr. J. H. Brooks had this moved over and made into his office, and he had a very beautiful, pretentious frame home erected on the corner.

It is now opportune to insert this item that Merta Sonner has written to me recently. In her letter she states, "I doubt if you have anything about the Lamp-Lighter. He would go around every night and light the corner lights. They were big, tall lights on high posts at each corner of Division Street. The one I remember most was at the corner of Division and Grand. I loved to wait there until he came and lighted it— don't remember who he was. The folks would send me to the store after school and I usually made it to that corner while he was making his rounds. They (the lights) were like the street lights in old-fashioned pictures."

There is a sad story of the fatality of a little Bandy girl, daughter of Brack Bandy, a prominent citizen. She was a pupil in the old schoolhouse. I learned of it when I was a child and her sister Ruby Bandy was my classmate. Now at this date Roxy Snyder has told me the probable cause of this terrible accident. She said it was fashionable then to wear on rainy days coats with capes, known as "McIntoshes"; and the Bandy child was wearing one when she left school that day. It was raining, with a very brisk wind blowing. Apparently the violent wind lifted the little girl's cape, covering her face and head, and she did not see or hear the oncoming train as it was rounding the curve back of the school. Just as she started across Division the train struck and killed her. Parents of schoolchildren for years afterwards warned them to be very cautious in crossing the tracks; for in those early days of Carterville there were many trains both day and night.

Now, more about J. H. Brooks, M.D. A native of Cobden, he came to Carterville in 1894. He was one of the first to recognize the value of the X-ray machine, according to a printed record by J. F. Wilcox in 1905 which further states, "His laboratory is fully equipped with all up-to-date machines for full electric and X-ray treatment." He was elected mayor in 1905. He was not a horse-and-buggy doctor but drove about in his classy, shiny red automobile to make his calls. The citizenry of the town dubbed it "Dr. Brooks' little red devil," for it scared the horses and frightened the cows. I know of one instance when it even alarmed a woman frightfully, living near the engineering building (now Jones Electric). This woman, the late Mrs. Pierce (Mary) Boswell, related to me prior to her death in January 1970 her fearful story in these words:

"I looked out the south window of my cottage, on Jersey Street facing East Illinois, expecting my young husband home from work on the J. J. Hunter building, and saw the strange contraption coming towards the house. It had nothing pulling it or nothing pushing it, and I was very scared. When Pierce came home he said I was as white as a sheet and explained it was Dr. Brooks in his new automobile." This was 1902, and the Boswells had just moved into Carterville a short time previously from the country south of town.

South Division Street boasted of two very nice jewelry stores in the early 1900's. One was that of C. E. Owen which had actually been established some years before; however, an earlier one was managed by Joseph Dodd inside the front entrance of Elles Store Company. Mr. Owen sold out to Harry Armstrong prior to 1914. Harry's father, John T. Armstrong, from Mound City took it over about 1923 and Harry set up a separate store in Marion.

The other jewelry shop was owned by J. W. Freeman, who came here from Golconda. He wore a long beard. I recall that a notable feature of this store was a long, massive wall clock near the front window, with its big brass pendulum. Even the schoolchildren timed themselves by it daily to and from school. Prior to Mr. Freeman's death, George McGonagil had his insurance business in the same store building south of MacKellar's bakery, and the clock remained on the same wall. When he sold his insurance business to Don Gentry Agency he said the deal included the clock. Mrs. Wilma Hampton of that agency has just told me that, after Larry Wimp moved this clock to Gentry's new colonial-type building, she found a card lying in the bottom of the clock which read, "The last time this clock was cleaned was when Orville Hodge cleaned out the State of Illinois." The reader can draw his or her own conclusion as to its source. Be that as it may, Wilma went on to say that George McGonagil still comes regularly to wind this unique, very beautiful clock which is a conversation-piece for customers who come into the office.

The jewelry store owned by the late Lloyd Harvel was housed in the building occupied so many years by both Owen and Armstrongs.

In the same block on the same side of South Division was Rice's Drug Store It is noteworthy to mention that there were three up-to-date drug stores in Carterville doing good business at the same time for many years. It was in 1892 that V. Rice from Benton set up his store with a brand-new stock of the necessary supplies. I remember especially the fine perfumes and colognes. His attractive neice, Fay Rice, whom he reared had access to the varied supply and was the envy of many teenage girls, me included, with her freedom and privilege to get from the glass case on the counter any fragance she desired, without the usual measurement of grams of the expensive sweet odors. Druggist Rice's tall, stalwart son, Hiram, had a printing shop on East Illinois where the Christian Science Church is now. He was the expert trap-drummer in the noted Sizemore Concert Band.

There were other stores of note south of Rice's about that same period, namely, Clark's Variety and Lofland's Harness Shop. I loved to go into the former to gaze at the beautiful dishes and particularly the exquisite "parlor" and banquet lamps on brass footings with large, flowered globes. About 1904 Mr. and Mrs. Wright bought Clark's, and my father bought a lovely large lamp with a cylindrical base as a Christmas gift for my mother, which I treasure to this day. The globe had hand-painted purple clematis. The price, $5.00, believe it or not, but deemed expensive at that time. Practically all homes had parlors then, and it was fashionable to set such a lamp on a center "stand-table" for admiration and to light occasionally the kerosene wick, with utmost care not to break the glass chimney or the globe. The parlors were especially reserved for company (guests).

I remember Mrs. Nancy Lofland, who kept the harness shop several years after her husband's death. The business was lucrative and the store was in close proximity to the town well and watering trough where the farmers gathered on coming to town. There was a need for the various leather trappings sold there. It is said that Montgomery's saloon in the same block attracted a lot of customers with an organ grinder and a dancing monkey and tin cup, so near the old town pump. On the wall of this building can still be seen the large painted letters: "MONTGOMERY'S PLACE— SELZ AND ROYAL BLUE."

This now brings me to the livery and feed stables that had sprung up in town. The first of record, according to Good-speed's *History of Gallatin, Saline, Hamilton, Franklin and Williamson Counties of Illinois,* 1887, was that of Irvin M. Walker and Mr. J. Stocks, which they erected in 1884; but in 1886 the former became the sole proprietor, averaging six buggies, one spring wagon and seven horses. Later Mr. Walker sold his entire interest to W. J. (Josh) Walker, his brother. They were brothers to J. V. Walker and Warren Walker, noted early Carterville merchants. This livery stable was located where the present Frost Furniture Store stands, and remained in business into the second decade of this century.

John Murphy, a native of Anna, Illinois, came to Caterville in 1882 and followed teaming and farming until 1894, when be began feeding mules for the Carterville Coal Company. In those early mining days many mules were needed to pull the loaded pit-cars in the shaft mines to the cages to be hoisted to the top and dumped into railroad cars. In 1900 he invested his earnings in the livery business and had taken Royce E. Cash as a partner. After three years they sold the business to W. B. Miller, but a year later Murphy bought back a half-interest. Royce Cash perhaps is better remembered as a very successful road construction contractor, in the East, who about thirty-five years after leaving the livery business returned to Carterville, his native town, with his heavy equipment and gravelled the Oakwood Cemetery streets, also seeding the entire acreage of it with blue grass as his memorial to our town.

In 1907 J. Wesley Hayton had come to Carterville from the Hayton settlement south of Crab Orchard Creek and bought the Murphy and Miller Livery, which he operated until he and his brother Maurice established in 1914 Hayton Motor Sales on South Division Street, distributors for Paige, Moon and Grant automobiles, later the Studebaker and Oldsmobile. "Wes," as he was familiarly called, had a beautiful black mare named "Daisy" and on Sunday afternoons, while proprietor of his livery stable on North Division Street—now the site of the American Legion building—would take his best girl friend, Zella West, who became Mrs. J. W. Hayton, buggy-riding with high-stepping "Daisy" hitched to a swank, cut-under, rubber-tired buggy. His good friend George Watkins, the popular barber, would rent a similar fashionable horse-drawn vehicle and take his bride to be, Zona Cash, for a long afternoon drive. Both couples, so beautifully dressed, looked so gay and charming, as I recall, when they drove by my girlhood home.

The livery stables did a healthy business to alleviate transportation problems for people in many walks of life. This was before the building of the hard roads. Mine officials from distant cities often obtained livery "rigs" to drive to the various mines north of town, Madison 8 (Dewmaine) and 9 (Colp), also Clifford (Big Muddy Coal Company). One noted official in particular, B. H. Carol from St. Louis, so fastidious in dress, came into town by train and stayed overnight at the Roach boarding house across from the old mill. Several young men and women were employed in the mine offices and large merchandise stores at Dewmaine, Colp and Clifford, and commuted daily by the jitney service (5c each way)—later called taxis.

"Wes" Hayton loved children and young people. Two occasions stand out for me while he was in the livery business. One winter, I think it was 1912 or 1913, a group of high-school girls and boys hired him to take us on a sled-ride one night to Herrin. The sled was a wagon bed on runners. The snow was packed and icy, but he had placed a lot of straw and provided ample heavy buggy robes to keep us warm. Everything went well until, as we were returning through Hurricane Creek bottom, northeast of town, the horses stopped and he "declared they had balked and he didn't know how long we would have to wait." The night was pitch black, and most of us were scared. Finally, with a pleasing chuckle of laughter—he had a great sense of humor—he tapped the team with his driver's whip and the horses pulled forward, to our sighs of relief. Another incident happened just before the high-school classes closed in May, 1914. Our Senior Class (1914) hired him to take our class and the Junior Class on a hayride that beautiful evening to a carnival in Carbondale, On returning that dark night through the old covered bridge over Crab Orchard Creek, again the team stopped "stock-still" in the middle of the gruesome and often-referred-to "haunted" bridge. But after a few moments of listening to our screams and pleas, "Wes," guffawing with laughter, urged his team homeward.

Other reminiscences of horse-and-buggy days stand out. I remember seeing Mr. J. B. Samuel and his beautiful wife, Dell, with their family in his fine surrey "with the fringe on top" going for a ride over the dusty streets in town, especially on Sunday afternoons. My grandfather, W. E. Sizemore, who lived a short distance from the north corporation line at the noted Sycamore Crossroads, also treated his family (wife and daughters, Eva and Ava) to such wholesome recreation as driving into town in his own fringed-on-top carriage.

There was a market for wild horses even after the turn of the century, and I remember some men in our neighborhood who purchased these direct from the railroad cars at the depot here after shipment in boxcars from the Western plains. The prices were reasonable, and many a farmer or farm boy enjoyed training these fiery animals to make them docile for farm work or even buggy horses.

Cecil W. Bishop—Runt, as he prefers to be called—links

in with the "metamorphosis" of Division Street in more ways than one. He came to Carterville from his home town, Anna, Illinois, in 1907 to operate the town's first picture-show known as the "Nickelodeon," situated just south of the Vick Drug Store. Miss Josie Gunster, who later married Royce E. Cash, played the piano and sang during the showing of those early silent movies. Not so long ago he told me that he had hired Vinnie McEwan, a popular young girl ,to sing with Josie's accompaniment; and after her first night's rendition he took her home after the show. This made her mother angry, and she stopped Vinnie from singing again at the movie. So Josie got the double job of singing and playing. Sometime later Bishop and Russel Crain, a home-town fellow, operated a moving picture-show across the street in the same building with the May Clothing Company, Leo and Monroe Crain, owners. These Crain brothers had succeeded two earlier Jewish clothiers, Olian and Landau from St. Louis.

In 1911 Mr. Bishop established his own tailor shop where cleaning, pressing and repairing could also be done. This was near the Walker Livery Stable. An efficient helper to him was another home-town young man. Cecil Gilkey, who later established a cleaning business in Herrin. There was another tailor shop in town about that time owned by a Mr. Norman, but with "Runt's" aggressive competition this man moved to Marion. Mr. Bishop continued in the cleaning and tailoring business until 1922. He was city clerk from 1915-1918. He became postmaster of Carterville in 1923, serving ten years. Before rising in political fame he worked as a coal miner, also was a telephone lineman and a professoinal football and baseball player and manager.

I remember the Carterville ball diamond in the Henry (Hank) Phillips field with its high tarpaulin-like fence surrounding it, where the present VanWyck Square housing is located. And once the famous St. Louis Browns came for a match game with the Carterville Tigers on a Sunday afternoon, even though Sunday ball games were quite controversial in the town at that time. He has recently informed me that

73

the St. Louis Cardinals played the team here in 1927 when Lloyd Bevard was manager, and furthermore, for two successive years Runt himself managed the Colp (all colored) Tigers.

After resigning as postmaster, Bishop joined the Lions' International as special representative traveling in every state of the union organizing new clubs, revitalizing others. He served as Lions' District Governor through 1932-1933 and is now the number one District Governor in the State of Illinois.

It was in 1940 that Mr. Bishop was elected to the Seventy-seventh Congress of the United States. He was this district's representative for seven terms ending in 1954. In 1955 and 1956 he was Assistant Postmaster General. From 1957 through 1960 he served as a member of Governor Stratton's Cabinet in the State of Illinois. Since his retirement in 1960 his great hobby has been golf, and he remembers with pride playing with President Eisenhower on the famous Burning Tree Golf Course, a green especially for Congressmen and high government officials in Washington, D. C. He has met and hobnobbed with many famous people. Vivid in his memory is Charles A. Lindbergh, who came to his home in Carterville in 1926, just about a year before his famous flight, to make arrangements for a field south of town to take up passengers the next day while on a barnstorming tour here. Mr. Bishop gave his consent for his young son, Jack, to take a short flight. "Runt" is also proud of the fact that, since 1960, he has headed the Williamson County Chapter of the American Cancer Society.

It was a memorable occasion when a special farewell affair was held in the spacious concrete-floored salesroom of Hayton Motor Sales for the newly elected Honorable C. W. (Runt) Bishop to Congress, the only man from Carterville ever chosen by the people of the fifteen counties of the 25th District of Illinois—a district which includes coal, oil, silica and spar, cotton-raising, cattle and fruit, and with dairy farming and factories—as their representative. Hundreds of well-wishers were there, I remember. His wife, Elizabeth, shared the honor with him that evening in 1941 before they departed by train for the nation's capital.

The Hayton salesroom a few years later became Phillip Tregoning's Garage and Texaco Station—another significant change on the Division Street thoroughfare.

Just south of the Zimmerman Building is a notable edifice bearing the name "B. H. Carter." It was erected by the son of Laban Carter, whose name our city bears. It was first used as a saloon by Barney Carter, but when the town was voted "dry" it was used for other enterprises, notably various restaurants and a movie theatre. At present Rushing's 5c to $1.00 store occupies its entire space.

After the days of Bishop's "Nickelodeon" the picture-show business thrived for many years in the town. George ("Red-Peck") Adams had a movie theatre on South Division approximately where the Modernell Beauty Shop is now. He named it "Bonita" for his wife. Later it was sold to John Marlow of Herrin, but Fritz Koennecke was the manager. Mr. Koennecke had had a varied career. He had set up in business as a baker in the town in 1891. In 1899 he formed a partnership with his brother-in-law, James Donaly, in the Donaly Koennecke Coal Company, the mine located near what is now known as Colp. The Bonita Theatre was a most popular place for entertainment and had a great patronage. "Squat" (Ray) Richardson, Sr. and his brother Gary were the competent operators of the projector. Lena Hampton (Zimmer) was ticket seller. Sina Hadfield McCabe played the piano during those silent movies, and in between the viewing of the shows she sang on stage for added entertainment. After six years at this, the coming of the talkies ended the need for her music performances. The Bonita burned to the ground in 1928.

In the early 1930's J. W. Hayton opened up the Hayton Theatre in the B. H. Carter building, where movies could be enjoyed for 10c admission. Wes had a generous heart and often let many underprivileged children in free. By this time the talkies were becoming popular, so Wes hired Ray Richardson (Squat), Sr. who had been working in Murphysboro, to run the new-fangled and difficult projector. Mr. Richardson continued to handle this intricate job as long as Hayton had a theatre. Some years later J. W. built an up-to-date theatre building on the old Bonita lot. He had no racial prejudice, although this was a controversial subject during the construction of the building. He prevailed, however, with his open policy extended to patrons from Dewmaine and Colp. Many outstanding civic programs were given on the large stage, especially honoring veterans and home-town boys in service in World War II and the Korean conflict. Many home-talent plays were also given on the stage.

Mr. Hayton died of a heart attack in 1958. He will long be remembered for his service to this community and as a friend to the friendless. He was elected mayor for several different terms. A number of streets were paved and water and sewer lines installed during his mayorality.

He was elected president of the Williamson County Fair Association in 1945 and served in that capacity until 1954. He had been a member since 1925, a period of thirty-one years. During this span he and his associates saw the Williamson County Fair bring to Southern Illinois the First Night Show in Southern Illinois, First Horse Show in Southern Illinois, and the First Night Races in Southern Illinois. He still maintained his love of horses and most every year attended the Kentucky Derby in Louisville with Attorney Hosea Skinner, another fancier of horses.

Mayor Hayton and Hon. C. W. (Runt) Bishop both personally greeted President Harry S Truman when he came through Carterville via motorcade along South Division Street on his scheduled route to Herrin on his campaign tour in 1948. Schools were dismissed and the streets were lined with children and adults all along the way. The dignitaries followed the route east on Grand Avenue. Several residents with movie cameras took pictures. An outstanding scene shows "Wes" in a dapper suit and hat with cane on his arm, as if turning over the "keys of the city" to the President, a token of honor extended for including this small city in his campaign itinerary.

MacKellar's Bakery succeeded Joe Stalcup's Bake Shop, and both used a horse-drawn bakery wagon to drive in all sections of town to sell or deliver their fresh-baked products. I remember the Stalcup one particularly. John MacKellar started in a small way after he came from Scotland about 1908, but it became one of the largest and most complete bakeries in Southern Illinois. His famous Butter-Krust bread was shipped in the 1920's to neighboring towns by express and truck every day. John Webber was the truck driver. Carl Wallace, still a Carterville resident, worked there when "Cy" Moore was shop foreman, and has some interesting pictures of the old bakery in its early heyday which show the old "Dutchess-Dough Rounder," the round drawer storage bins, the "Century" dough-molder and the old St. Louis Berken-bosh Oven. Carmen Purnell, Edna Ardery (Sizemore-Berry) and Mable Radcliff and Troy Barwick were employes also.

Mr. MacKellar became a mayor of Carterville. G. D. Wallace has written these words about him: "Of Mr. MacKellar I have one interesting item, that is his original hand-bill the time he run for mayor of Carterville. I made the drawing of him for the hand-bill. But it was Mr. MacKellar who came up with his own slogan of 'The man with his hands in his own pocket instead of the other fellow's.'" The MacKellar Bakery was just north of the Y-C Shop. The Margrave Brothers of Herrin became owners of the bakery in the late 1940's and operated it for a while, before closing it out. At present the Ascheris Bake Shop, north of Frost Furniture, is the only bakery in town.

John MacKellar, although childless, was fond of children. It was a custom that became a tradition for him to act as Santa Claus at the big Christmas tree, always set up in the center of the town square, handing out treats to the children after their singing of carols around the yule tree. Many times he visited each schoolroom, taking candy gifts to the children.

Mrs. Mary MacKellar, his wife, was expert at knitting. I have seen her many times standing out in front of the bakery greeting people who passed by and never dropping a stitch during their friendly chit-chat. During World War I she taught a group of Carterville ladies to knit khaki yarn sweaters and wristlets for the American Expeditionary Forces, and it is to her credit that Carterville met its quota of these items to be sent to our soldiers.

Now it is apropos to mention the millinery stores. The Y-C Shop, in the Axie Norton building south of MacKellar's, was owned by Miss Gus Young and Mrs. Ruth Norton Crain, who carried on successfully—notably between 1910 and into the 1920's, when hand-made hats for women and children with their beautiful ribbons, flowers and feather trimmings were the vogue of the day. The shop also sold fashionable suits and coats. Mrs. Crain's mother had owned this business prior. But due to the heavy responsibility of operating the Norton House and the Carterville Hotel at the same time, she sold it to the Y-C partnership. The building now is occupied by the Rowatt Laundromat.

Millinery stores were common in the early days of the town. It is known that Elles Store Company, before the turn of the century, employed a Mrs. Lavender as manager of its millinery department situated at its southeast corner entrance, where beautiful hats would attract the fashionable shopper. Later a Mrs. Alexander was the milliner in charge. I remember my mother buying for me a large bedecked ribbon hat, maroon color, for me to wear to a house party in Carbondale about 1909. In this department was a very large framed oval mirror that could be wheeled about, the kind so rare now in the antique market.

Miss Lizzie Crain had a well-patronized millinery business on the east side of South Division where her neice Ruth Porritt Tuberville assisted her with Miss Mae Deason and sister, Pearl (Mrs. Locket) Love. A humorous little story I must interject here. It was back in 1912, and willow-plumed hats were high-fashion, the plumes often costing as much as $18.00 alone. Two beautifully dressed young belles of our town, Lizzie Crain and Belle Winning, were taking an autumn Sunday afternoon stroll in my neighborhood in the northwest part of town, as was customary in those days. One of them—our little city's classiest milliner, Lizzie Crain—wore a big, black velvet hat crowned with a large, gorgeous plume that waved gently as she walked. The street was tree-lined. Quite unexpectedly an overhanging twig snatched the fragile, curly plume, dropping the hat at her feet. With a laugh, though chagrined, the milliner picked it up, fixed it back on her head, and they both resumed walking down Prosperity Street.

Mrs. Dell Cox (wife of Jeff Cox) also was a popular milliner. About the time of World War I, Miss Margaret Clark (now Mrs. Willie Hastie) came from DuQuoin as a professional milliner for Mrs. Cox. In the early 1920's Lelia Caplinger (now Mrs. Maurice Hayton) bought the Cox Millinery Store, which also carried a fine line of ready-to-wear for ladies. It was then known as Lelia's Shop.

There have been several changes in recent years at that location. It was here that Rosalee Hooker opened her store for infants' wear and baby gifts, naming it "Sharon's Shop," for her own young daughter. When she moved to larger quarters across the street and expanded the merchandise into a department store, the name became "Hooker's." Two other firms occupied the space vacated—the first a paint and wall-paper store owned by Mrs. Matt Steffes, the second by Crosthwaites. The bank needed this building in its remodel-ing program; the latter also needed another location for its lovely stock of gifts, paints and wallpaper. So Crosthwaites obtained the former X. M. Huss building north of the J. V. Walker, remodeled it and moved into it forthwith.

The present Priddy Cafe, the Tiny Tot Shop and the new CandyCane Miniclean in the 100 South Division block have some history also. For a number of years Theodore Anastaplo had a confectionery and lunch room known as "The Thrill," where the cafe is now. Mr. and Mrs. Joe Simonton opened up a variety store in the 1920's where the Tiny Tot is, later moving into the larger building north of it (the original Bracy-Hardware location) and now occupied by the Miniclean firm.

79

This building is owned at present by Mrs. Alberta Valentine. The Ed Clutts Shoe and Repair Shop and Spears Barber Shop are well known today on South Division, having been here for a number of years in this same block. A Kodak picture dated August 1, 1930 sent to me not so long ago shows G. D. Wallace at the roll-top of the original J. W. Russell studio on South Division Street (near the old town pump). Another picture of him was taken later showing him dressed in U. S. Marine Corps uniform, photographic section. Mr. Wallace occupied this old studio as photographer in his own right, prior to leaving Carterville, before World War II. The building was later taken over by George Watkins Cleaning Service. This was during the Depression years. Cecil Gilkey, Edna Sizemore Berry and Russell Talley all worked in it with Mr. and Mrs. Watkins. In 1942 Todd Taylor bought out Watkins. Today Talleys Cleaners operate their business there. In addition to managing this nice shop Russell has had made an interesting collection of pictures of early Carterville which are framed beautifully and displayed attractively in the front of his establishment.

As I reflect further on other changes on South Division I must mention the most recent one: the demolition of the Colp-Arnold Flouring Mill in April 1971, an historic landmark, now no more. The adjacent brick building still houses the Carterville Lumber Company, Inc., which location has had three other predecessors, namely the Colp-Arnold Lumber Company, the McCabe-North and the Steffes Lumber Company. The smaller brick adjoining building just south was the office of A. H. Wiswell of the Carterville Lumber and Fuel Company. Many years later it served as the office of the Venable Oil Company. The Matt Steffes Lumber and Construction Company is just to the rear facing Brown Street.

Another landmark on North Division Street is Holmes Garage. The two massive brick pillars over its driveway in front have recently been torn down in preparation for the widening of North Division. However, the building remains intact and is used for storage of boats, as Carterville is now in a noted recreation area due to Crab Orchard Lake. The Holmes enterprise was organized by two brothers, G. H. and E. C. Holmes, in 1914, and their business in the Thompson building by 1916 had grown so extensively that in the fall of 1917 they bought three lots farther north on the east side of the street, just a block from the J. B. Samuel building, and began a new building (the present structure). After the deaths of these two brothers, G. H's widow, Stella Holmes, sec'y-treasurer of the firm, continued to manage the business until her death in 1969. This garage was known all over Williamson and adjoining counties by automobilists. It had been an agency for both Overland and Oakland cars; in later years, a Phillips 66 station.

Not far from the Holmes Garage location—in fact, about where the American Legion Home stands—was the site of an early blacksmith shop of a pioneer settler in this area who set up his lap-boarded smithy before the town began. He was William C. Stover, great-grandfather of G. D. Wallace. Mr. Wallace has stated that it was either begun or was finished in 1855-1857. Certainly, with the needs of that time and with the discovery of coal later and the coming of the railroad with many spurs and switches so necessary, other blacksmith shops sprang up. Have you ever heard of Horne's Go-Devil? It was a forerunner of today's automobile and was constructed in Stover's shop, possibly between 1895 and 1900, being made of 90% wood and 10% metal. Mr. Wallace has also stated that Frank Sizemore, the noted band conductor and barber, told him he had seen this "Go-Devil Contraption" behind Stover's old shop, although it was in disrepair, and that photographer J. W. Russell had made a picture of it. I do know Mr. and Mrs. Frank Sizemore lived in a small cottage in the 1890's where Holmes Garage stands. Besides being a blacksmith Stover was a "J. P." in the area and conducted some of the trials regarding the bloody vendetta. His daughter, Amanda, married David Wallace, who was G. D. Wallace's grandfather. She, being very outspoken, had her share of people who did not like her, but she held her head so erect that the town referred to her as "The Duchess." Roxy Snyder has substantiated this, and remembers how she used to entertain the neighborhood children with interesting stories. One time Mr. Wallace was taking the "Duchess" to the depot to board a train to a distant city to attend a Pythian Sister lodge convention—there was a strong organization of the Knights of Pythias and the Pythian Sisters here at that time—and Mrs. Wallace, beautifully dressed in her rustling silk taffeta costume, walked so sedately and proud that the children nicknamed her "Duchess." They liked her very much and she was very kind.

After the village of Carterville started, Jimmie Jones, brother to E. C. Jones an early trustee, had a blacksmith shop at the corner of North Division and Virginia Avenue, now the location of the Dr. Shively building. He was a specialist in circling wagon wheels with iron rims. He had a two-wheeled cart he kept supplies in, and he would let the neighborhood children run up and down the dusty Virginia road in summertime pulling this cart behind them. This they considered great fun, even though they would have to be scrubbed from head to toe before their mothers would allow them to get into bed at bedtime.

Another notable blacksmith shop was the one owned by George Davie, which was just east of the Illinois Engineering Building, commonly known as the City Hall, on West Illinois Avenue. Mr. Davie set up his shop probably around 1901 or 1902 and maintained his business there until possibly 1916. The Davies' reared a neice, Edith Metz, who was a classmate with me all through the grades and high school. After graduating she taught at the South Side School in 1914-1915, prior to her marriage. After the Davie family left Carterville, Aus Armstrong did a good business there. Harry Flickinger had a blacksmith shop beginning in 1905, between the bank building and the city hall, for many years on the lot where the VFW is now located. It later burned. I must mention also George Stone, an early blacksmith whose smithy was situated on a plot of ground where the J. B. Samuel lumberyard was later located, according to information given to me by the late Leo Watson.

On the threshold of the front door of the former city hall, now the Carterville Public Library, is an iron door-plate with the molded words: "ILL. ENGINEERING CO." I don't know whether this historical plate was forged by a Carterville blacksmith or not, but it could have been.

Just "kitty-cornered" from the city hall at the junction of Pine Street and West Illinois stood a big, barn-like frame building for many years. It was unpainted, but it was the headquarters of the H. G. Caplinger Ice Company, which flourished so prosperously in the early 1920's. There was also another ice-firm operated by John Hundley that enjoyed a good business. Both had horse-drawn ice wagons that went all over town delivering the large ice-chunks handled by strong men with ice-hooks direct to the galvanized lined refrigerators or ice-boxes, set usually on the back porches, where perhaps a hole through the floor let the melting drippings escape. However, many customers kept a large pan underneath to catch the drip, and oftentimes the water overflowed on the floor, causing much inconvenience to the housewife. But every resident that could afford an ice-refrigerator felt it a much greater convenience over the oldfashioned way of hanging butter and milk, sometimes fresh meat, in buckets suspended on ropes down into a well or cistern, to prevent spoilage. And children loved to grab small bits of ice off the delivery wagon while the ice-man was indoors. Each looked forward daily to the time he would make his rounds.

Caplinger's ice-house some years later was used as a garage for car repairs. It was torn down in 1968 and a nice brick apartment building was erected by John McCoy, who maintains his barber shop and insurance business downstairs. This location is not far from where the first depot of Carterville was placed on Olive Street at the railroad crossing.

Carterville is proud of its beautiful Fire and Police Station, with its ultra-modern fire equipment etc. It faces the Carterville Public Library, each adding to the prestige of this section of West Illinois Avenue.

The library, established in 1965 as a tax-supported library, was originally started by the Carterville Business and Professional Woman's Club in 1949. Much credit is due Mamie Walker, Library Committee chairman, and Hazel Arnold as librarian. It became a charter member of the Shawnee Library System in 1965, whose administrative headquarters are located on the Greenbriar Road, just opposite the John A. Logan College, about one and one-half miles southwest of the city limits. The Carterville Public Library has had a tremendous growth since the city granted the old city hall for its use and it was moved to this location April 19, 1969. It serves the entire Tri-C area, Carterville, Cambria and Crainville. On April 23, 1971 its "Heritage Room" was officially opened as a reference and reading area. Of particular significance are the beautifully framed large maps printed from the original plats of Carterville, these donated by Donald Richardson, a native son now residing in Chicago. The glass and molding are gifts of Helen Campbell, and framing gratis by Robert L. Pennock.

I have previously mentioned that it was in 1915, under the leadership of Miss Minnie Ferrell, daughter of Dr. H. V. Ferrell, first president of the Carterville Woman's Club, that a library was instituted and situated in the rear room of the Carterville State and Savings Bank. I remember going regularly to this library between 1915 and 1925 when Mrs. Mae (Jett) West and Mrs. Robert Thompson served as librarians. I have recently come across some interesting historical tid-bits published in the *Carterville Herald* by C. S. Coddington when editing this local paper.

They are as follows:

Carterville Herald, December 26, 191⁹

MANY BORROWERS

The number of patrons of the Carterville Public
Library is increasing steadily. There are now 718
book borrowers listed. There is a big demand for
books daily.

C. S. Coddington, Editor and Publisher
Svbscription $1.50 per year in Williamson County.
Elsewhere $2.00 payable in advance.

Carterville Herald, Friday, October 8, 1920

WOMAN'S CLUB TO
HAVE PIONEER DAY PROGRAM WEDNESDAY

An interesting program has been arranged for
the next meeting of the Carterville Woman's Club,
Wednesday, October 13. The afternoon will be
devoted to a review of pioneer day experiences in
Carterville. Talks will be given by members and
invited guests on "The Founding of Carterville,"
"The First Stores and Residences," "Pioneer Men's
and Women's Work," "Pioneer House and Furnishings and Market Day" and "The Work of
Pioneer Physicians."

It is significant to note at this point that Carterville Woman's
Club ladies were interested then in the heritage of Carterville, just as we are today as we begin to celebrate our Centennial Year!

It is reasonable to assume that the nucleus of the books
in Carterville's first library could have been volumes from
the old collection used by the high-school students in R. G.
Crisenberry's office. He served as the high-school superintendent from the fall of 1910 through 1916, a very scholarly
man, an able administrator who afterwards was elected to
the Illinois Legislature, serving for twenty-eight years. He is
also accredited with his work in raising the status of Southern
Illinois Normal University to Southern Illinois University.

Long before the Woman's Club library occupied the back

85

room of the bank, there was a small restaurant in it operated by "Daddy" Burke and his prim, neat wife, "Pauliny." Helen Peach vividly remembers that Mr. Burke often sat out in front in a "splint-bottom" chair tilted back on two legs with his brown cocker spaniel at his feet. "Daddy" was quite obese and "Pauliny" always wore big, round earrings in her pierced ears. What good soup Mrs. Burke made, too! Helen has said she and her sister, Ruth, were given fifteen cents each every mine payday by their father, "Poker Jim" Harris, and with a playmate, Hazel Gallagher, spent it three ways —5c to go to the movie, 5c for an ice-cream cone at X. Huss' Confectionery; and coming back by Burke's Restaurant for their other nickel, Mrs. Burke would empty a big bowl of the delicious soup into a little tin bucket which Ruth carried along for the purpose.

Helen's mother kept boarders and often had "show people." Once, according to Helen, there was a carnival in the city park, more commonly known as the "Grove," near the North Side School. Incidentally, the "Grove" contained many of the virgin oak trees at that time, and there was a beautiful frame double white gate underneath an arched entrance for the convenience of horse-drawn vehicles. On one side was built a stile of several steps for pedestrians' use. Helen has told a humorous story relating to that carnival. There was a big, fat woman known as "Jolly Alma" in the troupe. Whenever she walked to and from the show tent to the Harris home she carried a big umbrella raised over her, with a curtain stretched all around so people could not see her. And this spectacle amused everyone as she passed by crossing Pine, Virginia and Olive Streets along the short route.

Another incident Helen recalls is when two midgets, a man and his wife, came to Elles Store to demonstrate a line of thread the store carried. It was held in the back of the Dry Goods Department. This fascinating couple stayed a week at the Harris boarding house. Mrs. Harris provided a child's high-chair for the little lady at mealtime, and she also placed hooks to hang their clothes on within their reach on the wainscoated bedroom. But the greatest thrill of all to Helen was later, at the time she was given a beautiful replica of an old-fashioned iron cooking range nickel-plate trim, that could be actually used. Her older sister, Rhea, had written an essay in a contest on the "History of Elles Store Company" and was awarded this fine prize, but gave it to her little crippled sister, Helen. All the kids in town came to see it after Helen's dad set it up with pipe, etc., in a special shanty outside, and they had so much fun cooking on it. Dora Russell, now Mrs. Fern Hastie, from "way over" on Texas Avenue, was among those playmates and school chums who enjoyed this novelty stove.

It is timely to note that the Harris boarding house had been the George M. McNeil hotel that had seen Carterville's birth on December 18, 1871, with its post office established there —and from which he, Mr. McNeil, the first postmaster, had planned the original survey of the village, with his dream of a commercial section along Division Street between Grand Avenue and Anderson Street, with Illinois Avenue in between this area forming a "cocoon." figurately speaking. The building of the railroad across his original survey—with a convenient switch to the Old Dodd Slope mine at the edge of the Laban Carter farm, and a spur track to the Old Burr mine, deep, shaft, at the adjoining Elijah and Mary Peterson land—assured a booming business in the shipment of coal, which now brings me to the subject of trains and depots.

As previously stated, the first depot was located at the corner of Olive Street and West Illinois Avenue, where the Hastie Cement works is located. About 1910 a new depot with separate building, side by each, to handle the great amount of freight and express by the Illinois Central Railroad, had been built on the corner lot, where the present post office is now located, at the corner of East Grand and South Division. There were many tracks, known as the "yards," between these depots and the Carterville Flouring Mill to accommodate many of the switching freight trains, as well as the six regular passenger trains that passed through

Carterville daily—three passenger trains going south and three northward bound.

C. R. Tripplet, station agent, now retired, and his wife, Zula Gallimore Tripplet, have given me much first-hand information concerning the booming business handled through both passenger and freight depots between 1910 and 1958. The latter was the date the Carterville passenger depot "died" and its windows and doors were boarded up. Clinton Drummond took a picture of it and gave it to me for my authentic collection of historical photographs of Carterville.

Mr. Tripplett came to Carterville in 1916, taking up his new duties as the telegrapher and ticket agent for the Illinois Central Railroad.

W. T. Wright had served as station agent for a number of years until around 1916, when he was transferred to Carbondale. M. W. Sizemore had been freight and express agent from 1897 to 1902. Succeeding W. T. Wright was T. A. Gannon. Mr. Gannon was the station agent from 1916 until 1941, when he was transferred to the Herrin depot. In the meantime Mr. Tripplett was a telegrapher at the DeSoto depot, but returned to Carterville in 1941 as station agent succeeding Mr. Gannon. Mrs. Gannon remained here on her job as freight and express agent on the depot grounds until retirement.

Mr. Tripplett handled the very extensive Western Union business as well as taking care of the ticket-selling and the almost overwhelming responsibility of billing coal via the many coal trains passing through here daily. He has said sometimes there would be so many loaded coal cars that it was necessary to have a "puller" engine on the front and a "pusher" engine at the back to carry the long string of cars to their proper destination. The billings of coal from the deep shaft mines of Madison 8, 9 and 12 as well as the Old Burr and the New Burr (Burr C) were all handled through this depot. In addition, there were long coal trains from mines in Kentucky, sometimes with engine pulling and another pushing, chugging and roaring past the depot. There was a very fast train dubbed "Tango" which passed through here promptly each midnight, going through on high on its run to Paducah without a local stop and whistling very loudly, even waking townspeople. Loafers downtown often said, "I can't go home until Tango comes through, for if I did go to bed it would wake me up!"

Mrs. Tripplett, nee Zula Gallimore, daughter of Judge J. L. Gallimore, has told me about the morning mixed train, passenger and freight, which switched daily in the "yard"— that section having several tracks between the depot and the flouring mill. It was called "Uncle Joe" for its kind, elderly conductor, Joe Youngblood, who was so respected by everyone, and whom the boys and girls loved.

Zula's father, the Judge, commuted often on this train to and from his county judicial office in Marion. She said he liked to talk with his family at each breakfast-time about law, and often he would delay. Many times as he was hustling from their home, a short distance from the depot "Uncle Joe" would be standing by his train and hollering: "Come on, Judge, come on! You're making me late!" But one morning a very sad things happened, and the unwanted responsibility fell to Conductor Youngblood to go direct to the Judge's home and inform him of the gruesome tragedy. The Judge's oldest son, Hal, and three other senior high-school students, Roy Howell, Bradley Gilkey and Rufus Kemp, were all "hopping" the early mixed train that morning, and Rufus met a horrible injury due to the train running over his legs. Dr. B. F. Crain, as soon as possible, amputated both limbs on the Kemp kitchen table.

All of these boys were classmates of mine. This happened in the early fall of 1913, and through the generosity of the merchants and other kind friends, artificial limbs were obtained when healing was sufficient for fitting. The other boys in that class, Walter Snyder, Norman Russell and Cluster Yewell, went daily to the Kemp home on Anderson Street just across from the school and carried the wheelchair with Rufus up two flights of stairs and to the classrooms so that he would be able to keep up with the class. He graduated with us June 6, 1914, standing on his new legs to give his oration. He told me in May, 1966 when he had returned for the annual alumni reception, that on his graduation night his pain was most intense; for that was the first time he had tried standing so long on them. But there is a happier note to this story. He was given an office job in Fulton, Kentucky by the Illinois Central Railroad and held it as long as he lived. His death came in 1968, fifty five years after his boyish escapade.

I am sure it must be difficult, perhaps, for many newcomers to visualize the many trains that passed through Carterville during the prosperous mining days. But the many mines and the railroad, not omitting the "Old Street Car Line," were at the core of its prosperity—coupled with the integrity and the willingness to work of the citizenry, in keeping with the lofty and honest principles that are the heritage from our forebears.

In March 1918, a Southern Illinois Divisional teachers' meeting was to be held at the new Shryock Auditorium at Southern Illinois Normal University, and ex-President Taft was to be the outstanding speaker on the feature night. Of course, I wanted to go and hear him. I was not teaching then, but three of my close friends were Lena Beasley, Maude Spires and Gaynelle Dempsey. So we bought tickets at the depot to ride the train to Carbondale and planned to stay overnight with friends. It was a very windy day; and while we were waiting on the loading platform with many others for the train to arrive a gust of wind blew off Gaynelle's new, big, straw spring hat. It went tumbling along until it lodged at the feet of a traveling salesman. The train was whistling in, and as she ran hurriedly to retrieve her beautiful headgear we heard her laughingly exclaim: "God bless that man's big feet!"

During the summer terms at Southern Illinois Normal University in 1919 and 1920, several of our local teachers and myself commuted daily to and from Carbondale on the passenger trains, leaving here at 6:05 in the morning and arriving back at our depot at 12:05 P.M. By the next year we were afforded transportation with Eva Stover, a local teacher, in her Model-T Ford on the old Route 13 highway, not all of which was actually completed then.

Mrs. Tripplett has also given a significant insight on railroaders' communication by means of the train whistles, especially in the "yards." There was a meeting place— in fact, two important ones—west of town, the closer one at Fredonia station (where the tracks crossed the road to Cambria) and the farther one at Reed's Station Road north of the present "Sav-Mart" store. She said she soon learned by the whistles of the oncoming noon trains (two of them) at which station they expected to meet, one train to wait on the side track until the other safely passed by. She further stated that if the meeting place was Fredonia she knew it was time to put her biscuits in the oven, and they would be just right to remove piping hot in time for "Trip's" supper when he walked to their home at the corner of East Grand and Walnut Street. They still reside there, and the new post office faces their residence. It should be mentioned that the most noted whistle-stop occurred at this corner in 1968, when Julie and David Eisenhower were campaigning for the election of Richard Nixon. This is a fitting place to bring my narration of the "Metamorphosis of Division Street" to a conclusion, inasmuch as the entire "cocoon" has burst all the way open, analogous to "from Dam to Beersheba," and the revelation of this phase of Carterville's hundred years is now a matter of recorded history. But there are other pertinent facts to record which follow.

CHAPTER III

SKETCHES OF THE LIVES OF THE CO-FOUNDERS
OF CARTERVILLE AND CHURCHES

George M. McNeill

In the year 1865, men were coming home from the Civil War. One of these was a young man who had just reached his twentieth birthday on June 5, 1865 and had spent three years in the service of his country. He was at the Battle of Shiloh, Chickamauga, Sherman's March to the Sea, Burning of Atlanta, and others. He was the son of John A. and Wealthy Walker McNeill, who lived on a farm three miles east of "The Sycamore" for thirty-four years prior to 1865. This was George M. McNeill. George was their oldest son, and at the age of seventeen he replaced his sick father as a soldier in the Union Army and served to the end of the war. Illness also attacked him, and during the grand review at Washington, D. C. he rode down Pennsylvania Avenue in a hospital wagon behind his regiment, the 9th Illinois Infantry.

On September 6, 1866 he was married to Olive Herrin of Herrin Prairie. They settled on the farm where Carterville now stands and farmed this land for several years. The house and farm building were in the block where the old City Hall stood—now the Carterville Public Library. This house was also home of the first post office, year 1871. The railroad from Carbondale to Shawneetown passed through this farm, being built in 1870-71.

On March 21, 1871, a lease was entered into by George McNeill, his wife Olive, and Frank J. Chapman, Asgill Conner, and Andrew C. Bryden for ninety-nine years for this forty acres, second vein of coal, and minerals. This lease was active until 1943, when Peabody closed their mines in Carterville and it was cancelled. McNeill had Bundy and Beasley, surveyors, make a plat of his forty acres for town lots. This was registered in Marion on February 21, 1872, and Carterville was founded on this farm by McNeill.

His farm home was enlarged and remained the hotel for many years, which he ran until December 1879, when he moved to another farm at the southwest city limits. He rented this hotel for many years before selling.

Carterville was in the making several years before it was incorporated April 10, 1872, when the plat was made for McNeill. He gave his half of Division Street. The farmer on the east never added his part, and that is why Division Street is so narrow and about which McNeill was ever sensitive. The first name submitted for the town was George-town for McNeill; however, this could not be used as there was another town in Illinois by that name. McNeill himself suggested Carterville, as he had the privilege of naming the town.

George McNeill's first wife died in 1874. They had four children: Laura, Ada, Arthur, and Robert. Laura became Mrs. Ed Duncan, Ada married George Parsons, Arthur died at age 28, and Robert passed away in infancy.

In 1875 he was united in marriage to Miss Alice Trahbarger, who died in 1918. To this union six children were born: John B., Merta (Sonner), Fred, Flora (Craig), Guy, Ernest who died in infancy.

George Monroe McNeill died in Herrin on February 13, 1931, aged 85 years, 8 months, and 8 days. In early life he united with the Hurricane Baptist Church, which was organized in his grandparents' home and later united with the Christian Church of Carterville, where he was a member at the time of his death.

Laban Carter

Laban Carter, co-founder with George M. McNeill of the village of Carterville, was born in Stanley County, North Carolina, August 28, 1822, the son of Levi and Jane (Holt) Carter. The father of English stock, born in 1791 in North Carolina, went to Henry County, Tennessee in 1823, and bought two hundred-eighteen acres on which he passed his life. He died in 1845. The mother, a native of North Carolina, was born in 1791 and died in 1829. Laban, the only survivor of seven children, was only seven when his mother died, and with meager pioneer school advantages, he received hardly a common school education. He married Berrilia Jackson in 1854. She died in 1860. He became the owner of one hundred forty-eight acres in Henry County. On September 15, 1861, he married Nancy Snodgrass. Their children were Sarah J. (who became the wife of Samuel H. Bundy), Barnett H., Minnie D., Thomas E., and Maggie D.

In 1862, he enlisted in Company A., Seventh Tennessee Infantry, but was discharged on account of disability at Trenton, October 3, after five months of service.

In 1863, he came to Jackson County, Illinois and six months later moved to Franklin County. In the fall of 1864 he moved to Williamson County and bought one hundred acres of land in Carterville Precinct. He succeeded in locating a post office at Carterville in 1871, and the village that grew up around it was named in his honor. He soon added forty acres to his farm and in 1872 leased one hundred-twenty acres to the Carbondale Coal and Coke Company for ninety-nine years, or as long as the coal lasted; and at one time he owned four hundred and forty acres. He is said to have been an able businessman, also a stockholder and director of the St. Louis Coal Railroad. His two-story farm home stood for many years at the northeast edge of town not far from where coal had been discovered on his land. Besides having the town named after him, Laban Carter was generally regarded as the founder of the Methodist

94

Church here. His home was the center of early church activities; and here the Circuit Rider found a welcome, a bed for himself and food and shelter and care for his horse.

I have no information as to the date of Mr. Carter's death, but a yellowed, tattered front-page item of the *Carterville Herald* issue of January 19, 1919 gives an account of the death of Mrs. Nancy Carter on January 11, 1919 at the age of eighty years, three months, and four days. She was the widow of Laban Carter.

Historic Churches

There were two country churches in the pioneer days of Carterville Township not so far from the corporate limits of the village, which did a great deal to mold many lives for the betterment of the community at large. "Old Hurricane" was situated about a mile east, and "Foreville" Church was located some two or three miles southwest of Carterville. The former was organized in July, 1837 when a little group of Baptists met in the home of Matthew M. and Hester Walker. One of their daughters, Wealthy, present at the organization, later became the wife of John A. McNeill. Mr. and Mrs. John A. McNeill were the parents of George M. McNeill.

Outdoor meetings in a brush arbor were held in the summer of 1837, but by fall a log house was built near the Hurricane Creek. This was replaced later by a larger church building—frame. But it burned and a brick one was erected. A big windstorm (hurricane in its velocity) wrecked the brick building. Then a frame church was built in 1884. This old building was finally torn down and useable materials, including the big bell, were taken to Herrin and used in construction of the Hurricane Memorial Baptist Church. I remember attending my grandfather Sizemore's funeral in 1912, held in the old frame church situated in its shady grove of trees and adjacent cemetery. I recall stories that my mother related of their family walking through the Burr

Woods and across the Sim McNeill acreage to reach the church for regular divine services (as they were called) on the Sabbath when she was quite young. She also told of Charles and Mattie Cash, with their six small daughters and one son in regular Sunday morning attendance sitting on a front church bench while Mr. Cash (later proprietor of the Park Hotel) led the congregational singing using a tuning fork to give the pitch. Many of the early pioneer families lie buried in historic Old Hurricane Cemetery.

From· Hurricane Church several others of like faith and order were organized, notably the First Baptist Church at Herrin (1865), the Carterville Missionary Baptist Church (1886), and Pigeon Creek Baptist Church (1889)—the latter situated in what is now government owned Wildlife Refuge known as Crab Orchard Lake District.

Foreville Christian Church was organized in an old schoolhouse a few years before a frame church building was built in 1874. For two years services were held in an unfinished room with rough benches. As years went by the building was completed and painted. A basement and other improvements were added, with it becoming a model country church. It is known that Elder Henry Boles, a Christian preacher, preached in it. An interesting excerpt I have gleaned from "A Souvenir History of Williamson County" states: "The first religious services held in Carterville by Henry Boles were in 1871, a year before the village charter was granted. Elder Boles, a Christian preacher, held a revival in 1887 which resulted in two hundred conversions." I have found no record that the revival of that date was held in Foreville Church, but it is reasonable to assume it could have been. Anyway, in my youth, I've heard many old-timers refer to this very influential church.

The churches within the corporate limits of Carterville, with their dates of erection according to H. F. Wilcox's book (1905), are:

Methodist Episcopal Church, 1875, and afterwards
  a new one in 1899.
Presbyterian Church, 1885
Baptist Church, 1886
Christian Church, 1888
Catholic Church, 1895

The First United Methodist Church (formerly Methodist Episcopal), Carterville, has the distinction of being the first church founded in the town. It stood behind Hampton's Drug Store and faced Hickory Street. A church was built in 1875, and afterwards a new one in 1899 at the present Pine Street location. This building was remodeled in 1923. In 1949 the church burned. On that day the wedding of Julianne Harper was to have been held in the church, but it burned before the wedding. Then in 1949 the present brick building was built.

The Presbyterian Church (frame) with its unique steeple stood at the corner of Cemetery Street and West Grand Avenue. After it burned it was never rebuilt, but the loyal members purchased the former residence of Edward A. Elles on West Grand, converting it into a chapel which was dedicated on April 2, 1944, according to record in the *Carterville Herald*—at which time Fred Richart narrated the history of the church, dating back to the time when the Presbyterians and Methodists worshipped together in a building on Hickory Street. He recalled the pastors who had come and gone, including Rev. William M. Maxton, who came in 1900 and served for a number of years—a notable pastorate.

The Christian Church met the same ill fate in 1909 by fire, but by the next year a beautiful brick edifice was built at the corner of Pine Street and Virginia Avenue. An educational building was added about 1955. It serves a large congregation.

The Catholic Church on West Illinois Avenue burned to the ground about 1915 or 1916. It was never rebuilt.

Another prominent Church was organized in October 1904, known at that time as the Freewill Baptist Church; and the building stood at the corner of Idaho and Locust Streets. In 1915 it and the two-story parsonage next door were destroyed by fire. When the church was rebuilt it was located at the corner of Oak Street and West Grand Avenue and became known as the Grand Avenue Baptist Church. In June, 1971 this church was razed to make way for the construction of a new auditorium to join a two-story brick educational building built in 1960. The auditorium capacity will seat two hundred and fifty.

The First Baptist Church experienced a fire one Sunday morning during Sunday School in the fall of 1927 when someone shouted, "Fire! Fire!" The door was opened and Clyde Martin, Sunday School superintendent (also principal of the Carterville Grade School) jumped upon a table and got the panicky people quieted down. Little damage was done, fortunately. In 1957 the two-story educational building was completed and dedicated. Now at this writing (1971) plans are underway to construct a new auditorium, doing away with the present brick veneer one that has been in existence since it was constructed in a remodeling program in 1923. Which reminds me, the church no longer having a belfry, the big church bell was done away with. Its whereabouts is still a mystery. But I recall from childhood days the beautiful tone of that bell and the sweet soundings of the various other church bells in town on Sabbath mornings. There was a custom also of tolling the church bell whenever a church member passed away, as a mark of respect or memorial.

This church building still has evidence of cracked walls and loosened bricks caused by the earthquake of November 9, 1968.

This further reminds me of a record of another earthquake that happened in Carterville, as told to me by the late Mrs. Molly Keith and Mrs. Lina North. I had gone to interview them in 1964 regarding the early history of the Carterville

First Baptist Church. They both attested that an earthquake happened during a revival meeting there just a short time prior to 1895, when R. D. McGinnis, known as the "boy preacher," was holding a revival. He was much concerned about the complacency of the people, and he prayed aloud for an earthquake or something to happen to shake them up to their sense of Christian duty and to convict sinners. During an alter service an earthquake did happen, and one mourner was so scared she fell off the mourner's bench flat on the floor. Young Preacher McGinnis became their brother-in-law in 1895.

Many shoutings were witnessed during early revivals of this church. To the writer's knowledge, two saintly, shouting women, "Aunt" Sally Fox and "Aunt" Emmaline Corder, stand out in memory.

There were numerous evangelists who held revivals in the Protestant churches in Carterville after the turn of the century. Probably the most notable was the famous Billy Sunday, the converted baseball player, who spoke at a special afternoon service in the Methodist Church. It must have been around 1916 or 1917 when he was holding a big tent meeting over in Johnston City. I attended this service. He had already reached national fame both as a ball player and a preacher. One of his famous quotes is: "If you want your wife to act like an angel, don't treat her like the devil."

Baptismal services were conducted at the Zimmerman Pond before baptistries were built in the churches that practiced immersion. This pond was also known as the Colp-Arnold Lake. I remember attending one such occasion to see my father baptized. It was on a December day about 1905, when a skim of ice had frozen over the entire pond. He with the pastor broke the ice as they walked into the deeper water. Several were baptized that cold afternoon. This lake is shown on the early maps of Carterville between Dent and Zimmerman Streets near Pin Oak Creek on West Grand Avenue. The Maple Grove Subdivision is on part of its location. I have been told water from this body of water furnished power for the A. C. Hope electric light plant.

Other important churches in Carterville and dates of establishment are: First Church of Christ Scientist, 1908; Church of the Nazarene about 1915; First Apostolic Church about 1936; and The Bible Fellowship Church, 1948.

Old Hurricane Church
Organized in 1837, it became the "mother" of four Baptist churches in Williamson County, including First Baptist Church of Carterville, organized 1886.

Looking North on Division Street
Right foreground, Carterville Hotel and movie theater. Charles A.
Lindbergh stayed in this hotel about a year before his famous trans-
atlantic flight.

Park Hotel
Charles Cash, proprietor, with Mrs. Cash and their two daughters; the
men on porch are unidentified.

J. V. Walker & Sons Clothing Company Before 1910
Right center: George Watkins, clerk; Willard Love, clerk; Fred Walker,
eldest son of J. V. Walker.

Elles Store Co., in early 1900s
Foreground, l. to r.: Ed Elles; Miss Vida Brown, sitting; Arthur Baker,
demonstrating groceries. Note cashier's cage, and mannequins high
above counters.

CHAPTER IV

EARLY HOTELS SIGNIFICANT
IN DEVELOPMENT OF TOWN

Perhaps this is a most fitting time to relate some of the history of Carterville's early hotels, inasmuch as each in its own way contributed not only to the basic needs of shelter and board to the many important personages who helped develop the town, but also was significant in the school and social life of the community.

The first hotel was in the large two-story frame farm house of George M. McNeill and dates back to December 18, 1871, when the old post office of Fredonia, south of Cambria, was transferred to this home and the office was renamed Carterville. Mr. McNeill was the young village's first postmaster. The mail was received and delivered in this house, which also served as a hotel. The new Carbondale and Shawneetown Railroad, which later became the Illinois Central, crossed his forty-acre farm in a sweeping curve just south of his home. The track is still in use now for the few daily trains that pass through here. However, by the early 1900's there were six passenger trains daily, besides many freights, using this track and adjoining switches.

The house is just west of the old City Hall; the City Hall now houses the Library. The railroad built its first depot on the north side of the track, west of the hotel, the spot now occupied by Hastie Cement Company. It was from this depot that all freight and railroad supplies were handled. Many railroad men, business prospectors and mine officials alighted from the trains or departed, as the case may be, and were frequent visitors or guests at the McNeill Hotel. Coal having been discovered on the Laban Carter farm one-half mile east, and with the completion of the railroad and with an authentic post office, business boomed in Carterville. Later a spur track offshooted from this "main line" leading to the mine. It crossed North Division Street bordering what is now Heckel's Exchange building and "The Antique" shop. Asgill Conner, one of the founders of Carbondale, interested in the completion of the railroad with Andrew C. Bryden, mine manager for Mr. Carter, and with Agness C. Bryden, the mine bookkeeper, were frequent comers to the hotel in those early days.

Albert K. and Edward A. Elles, founders of Elles Store, were regular boarders. Their two brothers, Charles F. and Louis T. Elles, joined them in 1877 to form the Elles Store Company. They were from Belleville. Mr. Ed, as his employees respectfully called him, met and married Miss Kate Bevard, one of the employees of the hotel, while boarding there. So it had its era of romance! I am indebted to Merta M. Sonner, Jacksonville, eldest surviving daughter of George M. McNeill, for much information she has related to me, from which I have given the highlights of Carterville's first hotel.

The noted Park Hotel, owned by Charles M. Cash, father, of Lina North and Zona Watkins, both of Carterville and Ruth Bracy, now of Salt Lake City, Utah, stood where the home of Mabel Craig is located on South Division Street, and just opposite the Colp-Arnold Flouring Mill.

This large, spacious frame hotel had two stories, containing seventeen rooms, not including the parlor, dining room, kitchen and dishwashing room. In the late 19th century and early 1900, the four beautiful daughters, Lina, Ruth, Zella (now deceased), and Zona each had their specific tasks to do daily in making the hotel spic, span, and hospitable. The hotel not only catered to the traveling public, especially mine operators and officials from Chicago or St. Louis, but also to the numerous traveling salesmen known as "drummers," who came into town by train. A new depot had been built across the tracks east of the mill, near where the post office is now. Their trunks and baggage would be unloaded and would be hauled by a one-horse dray operated by the patient and kind, crippled drayman, Bennie Smith, direct to the "drummer's" salesroom in the hotel to be opened and displayed for the buyers who came from the Elles Store and other local stores to select shoes, clothing, ready-to-wear and sundry dry goods, materials, etc. to order. In later years the salesmen who sold to Elles would have their trunks drayed to the large department where Vida Brown and Jake Ford would make the selections of the latest fashions in ladies', children's and men's wear. Jesse Brown was the buyer for the shoes.

Mr. Cash, owner and proprietor, also did a thriving business at his cigar counter. In the dining room there were three tables always set with white linen tablecloths and matching napkins. Lina Cash North says she washed napkins every day, and they were cold-starched, ironed and folded in lily form and placed in the water glasses. The table set "special" for the "drummers" was the prettiest, she affirms. The second table was for the other transient roomers, while the third was for the family and the cooks.

The first Carterville High School graduating class, four girls and four boys, 1903, was feted at a banquet in high style in this dining room. Janice Lockie Searl, Holmes Beach, Florida, daughter of the late Clara Perry Lockie, member of the class, has recently written while going through some of her mother's papers she found the old 1903 banquet program which contained the menu and commencement exercises. Zella Hayton, who graduated a few years later, also has the banquet menu served to her senior class by the few early graduates who had organized the first Alumni Association of Carterville High School. She regards it as one of her most prized souvenirs. She remembers vividly the grand style in which it was served in the Park Hotel, J. W. Wheatly, manager. The class numbered seven girls. Mrs. Hayton recalls how important she felt to be banqueted in a hotel. The alumni at that time totaled only fifteen, which included the graduates of 1903, 1905, and 1906. Agnes Stewart was in the 1905 class.

It is of interest to read a copy of the seven-course banquet as follows:

Menu:
Oysters—Raw, stewed, fried, Heinz pickels, deviled relish.
Cold slaw, sliced tomatoes, young radishes.
Cold:
Chicken, ham, pickeled tongue, cranberry jelly, deviled eggs.
Salads:
Salmon, nut, potato, lemon tartlets, French rolls.
Cake:
Carmel, banana, chocolate, neapolitan ice cream, or french confectionery.
Fruits:
Oranges, bananas, apples.
Assorted nuts, Eden cheese, Delito crackers, coffee, coco, tea.

Mrs. North and Mrs. Watkins remember that marriages were sometimes performed in their father's hotel in the spacious parlor. One in particular was that of Oscar Peyton, a prominent young early merchant here, to Miss Kate Powell.

Mrs. Watkins says that when she and her sister, Zella, got big enough they had to wash the numerous dishes and used two washtubs for this purpose. She relates that once while doing this distasteful task both of them got mad and Zella grabbed a pound of butter and threw it in Zona's hair. They both had to stay home from a party that night.

Before this noted hotel met its sad fate by fire, Mr. and Mrs. J. W. Wheatley took over the management and operated it successfully for several years. Many residents wil remember the genial Wheatleys, parents of the late "Toodle" Lauder and Pauline Randal, Washington, D. C. Eileen Lauder Rice and her brothers, Frank and Fred, are grandchildren.

There was another large hotel that catered to the traveling public about the time the Park Hotel was in its heyday. It was the famed Thompson House, a pretentious two-story, many-windowed frame building with a dormer-windowed third story. Its location was at the corner of North Division and Virginia Avenue, where Corbitt's Texaco Station is now. It had a long front porch all across its east front. Carved bannisters added to its style of architecture, reminiscent of the "gingerbread" age in which it was built. Its owner, James T. Thompson, and his wife, known as "The Missus," extended gracious hospitality to all who sought its conveniences. Mary Barth leased this popular first-class hotel in 1903. Some years later two of Mr. Thompson's sons, Bob and Sandy, converted it into a general merchandise store, known as the Mercantile Company. Huge plate glass windows enclosed the large front porch, forming nice display places. The writer recalls an outstanding window trim of festooned white embroidery edgings with matching flouncing and insertion. In those days many wedding and graduation gowns were made by local dressmakers, using yards and yards of these materials in the feminine mode of the day. Ruth Washburn, granddaughter of the owner, says another feature was fine imported Irish linen tablecloths, napkins and towels. The late Tena Thompson was the daughter of the owner. Hazel Deason now widow of the late Dr. Green of Johnston City, was the bookkeeper. A tragic fire leveled it about 1914 or 1915, and it was never rebuilt.

In 1910, A. C. Hope had erected a large, angling, two-story brick building at the corner of South Division Street and East Grand Avenue, facing the ICRR, with the dining room entrance on Division Street. This site had been the spot some years before of a balloon ascension that attracted crowds. Mr. Hope named it the Alexander Hotel after himself. The Hope Electric Light Plant had become quite a successful enterprise for him here. According to an early account, published in 1905, arc lights were used for the streets, business houses and residences were well-lighted, and travelers said that Carterville was one of the "best lighted cities in Southern Illinois." There was a "drummer" room looking south towards the railroad, and a narrow viewing veranda all along this room joining the east wing of the building, where tired travelers coming off the numerous trains could rest, perhaps after being served delicious meals in courses in the dining room off the lobby. To reach the dining room (it was a forerunner of the "split-level" modern style) one descended three steps down into the dining room. Mr. and Mrs. J. Wes Hayton operated this hotel for a while after their marriage. Then, in the early 1920's, Mr. Hope sold the building to Axie Norton, who also operated the Norton House just across the tracks west of it—the former Dr. J. H. Brooks' pretentious home, with its rounded cupolas. Don Gentry's Agency is built on this location. This historic Brooks mansion was torn down in 1968.

It is timely to note that Mrs. Norton's daughter-in-law, Lizzie Norton, was noted for the annual quail suppers she served to special guests each autumn. Probably the longest operators of the hotel were Mr. and Mrs. Richard Waldron, who acquired it after Mrs. Norton's death. Mrs. Kate Waldron won much acclaim for the delicious family-style dinners, especially chicken and dumplings, also turkey, which she served regularly—drawing much patronage from many surrounding towns especially on Sundays. She also catered to school and church banquets and special parties.

This story cannot be complete without mentioning a very unusual guest in 1926, about a year before he became world famous as "The Lone Eagle," who flew the *Spirit of St. Louis* on the first non-stop transatlantic flight. Yes, it was Charles Lindbergh, who on his way from the South stopped in Carterville to do some barnstorming. The late Jack Bishop, son of Mr. and Mrs. C. W. Bishop, then a young lad, was one of his passengers in his "crate" on a farm south of town.

But, alas and alack, this hotel fell in disrepair and in its final years furnished room and board for elderly men! One July night in 1967, fire was discovered, and although several fire departments responded it could not be saved. Its gutted hulk was an eyesore to all who passed by; but its date, 1910, remained intact on the front west wall until the building was completely razed in the summer of 1969. Then came the erection there of the Carterville State and Savings Bank's new drive-up red brick building which, with the beautiful, tall white columns on its two fronts, resembles a very magnificent Grecian temple now.

So ended the historic era of hotels in Carterville.

Carterville State and Savings Bank After Reopening, 1931
Left to right: J. W. Hayton, Mayor; Leo Watson, cashier; Walter Rowatt,
president.

Carterville State and Savings Bank, about 1905
M. W. Sizemore, cashier; Alice Fleming, bookkeeper.

McKellar's Bakery
Edna Ardrey (Sizemore—Berry); and John McKellar, owner.

E. Beasley's Blacksmith Shop
Elmer Beasley, pointing to harrow; unidentified; David B. Bogard; Lewis Crowder; Aus Armstrong; unidentified.

CHAPTER V

A MUSICAL BAND IN CARTERVILLE'S SAGA:
THE FRANK SIZEMORE CONCERT BAND

This is a story of the early musicianship of Carterville's renowned Sizemore's Concert Band. For the older citizens who remember, may it be a nostalgic therapy of musical pleasure. For the younger folk and newcomers, perhaps it will create appreciation of the fading history of this town's former proud, talented and handsome band performers.

Matt Watson, when interviewed some months ago at his home at 202 James Street, Carterville, is the only living member of the original Sizemore's Concert Band. He said he played with Frank Sizemore, organizer and conductor, for twenty-three years and wore out three horns. He recalled that in November, 1909, Sizemore and his band were invited to St. Louis to play for that city's Centennial Celebration. The band had only eighteen members at that time, so Sizemore recruited seven other young musicians from Marion, Herrin, and Johnston City to make up the needed twenty-five to qualify to march in the big parade. There were three thousand, three hundred bandmen from all parts of the nation in the parade, and it took four hours to pass any particular spot marching five abreast. As Sizemore's band was passing the reviewing stand, Owen Miller, National Secretary of the Federation of Musicians, was in the stand and signaled to stop the parade. He came down from his box-seat and shook hands with Mr. Sizemore in recognition of the fine musicianship and excellent performance of his band. Mr. Miller, too, was a personal friend of Frank Sizemore, having come to Carterville when the Musician's Union, composed of Carterville, Marion,

107

Herrin, and Johnston City bands, was chartered here. Carterville kept the charter. The band was held an extra day in St. Louis and was the only band from Illinois that was invited to play the second day of the celebration.

On returning home, Frank Sizemore composed "The Pike's Parader's March" to commemorate the honor his band had received at the Centennial. His band soon learned to play it.

The band played at the many Fourth of July celebrations in our beautiful wooded City Park, which drew thousands of people from near and far at these annual affairs, as well as the yearly Labor Day festivities held in the mining area of Southern Illinois. Each year on Memorial Day, this Concert Band would head the "Decoration Day" parade leading to Oakwood Cemetery ... followed first by the Civil War Veterans, who rode in carriages, later in cars; and marching directly behind were the Spanish-American War Veterans. Later the Veterans of World War I joined the ranks of honored soldiers and sailors. Then marching in step came the numerous Lodge organizations, followed by the school children and various floats.

On Saturday afternoons, band concerts would be given at the intersection of Division Street and Illinois Avenue for the enjoyment of shoppers and children downtown. The band members looked so handsome in their winter uniforms of dark green with gold braid, or for summer performances dressed in dark trousers and white coats with brass buttons.

Frank Sizemore also conducted the County Band as they played for the annual Williamson County Fair for many years. He was proud of his record of service, either as conductor or a participant, there with many of his own band members for fifty-six years.

Daisy Hadfield and Dora Hadfield, widows of Robert and Dick Hadfield, both Hadfield brothers and a third brother, Joe, members of the original band, tell of the annual Thanksgiving celebrations where the band officers were elected for the ensuing year, and the bountiful noonday dinner served to the members and their families. They would always give an afternoon street concert, then assemble for supper followed

Carterville Band in City Park, Early 1900s
Back row, l. to r.: Tom Porrit; Will McEwan; Jim Taylor; John Rowatt; Jim Hutton; Dick Hadfield; Alex McCrae; Chester Taylor. Seated: Frank Sizemore, conductor; Ed Sizemore; Billie Swaar; Hiram Rice; Charlie Dunn; John King.

The Carterville Orchestra, Early 1900s
Seated, l. to r.: Jim Taylor; Dick Hadfield; John King; Josie Gunster, pianist; Alex McCrae; Robert Porrit; standing, Tom Porrit. Picture taken in Gunster Home.

In the Frank Sizemore Livingroom, 1909
Left to Right: Frank Sizemore, band conductor and composer; Henry du
Bois, stepson; Mrs. Frank (Lizzie) Sizemore, who was noted for her beau-
tiful needlework. Sheet music on piano is "Pike's Paraders," composed by
Mr. Sizemore to commemorate the Sizemore Concert Band's winning
first prize at St. Louis Centennial celebration, 1909.

by an evening dance in the Hall. These annual affairs were first held in the UMWA Hall in the old Thompson Building, above the present Heckel's Store. Later they assembled in the Herrin Eagle's Hall. When meeting in Herrin, the dancing lasted only until 11 p.m. in order to catch the "owl" street car home, it being the last car to run at night of the Coal Belt Electric Line, the terminal of which was at the end of the tracks on East Illinois Avenue between J. V. Walker's Clothing Store and Joe Kelley's Drug Store.

But that's another story about "THE OLD STREET CAR LINE."

CHAPTER VI

THE OLD STREET CAR LINE

It may seem unbelievable, but it is true that Carterville had a thriving street-car service, in the early 1900's, with electric cars shuttling daily on the hour every hour from 7 a.m. to 11 p.m. between Carterville, Herrin and Marion, the Tri-Cities in the heart of this noted Black Diamond Field of Southern Illinois.

The Coal Belt Electric Railway connected these coal towns with an interchange at "Fordville," now Energy, where for many years the company maintained its own powerhouse to generate the electric power for its trolley lines. In its later years the line abandoned the powerhouse and bought its service from the C.I.P.S. Company. The cars were propelled by electric power from electric overhead wires suspended from poles eighteen feet above the rails. The following story authenticates its beginning and traces its history until its demise almost twenty-five years later.

It was during E. B. Watson's second term as mayor of Carterville in January, 1902 (his mayoralty was from 1901 through 1904) that permission was granted by the City Council and approved for the electric line to be built by the Coal Belt Electric Railway Company.

According to the ordinance, the line of track was authorized to extend from the east boundary of Carterville to a point where Illinois Avenue crosses Division Street; and the company was allowed a period of one year to complete the construction of the track, and was to maintain and operate it for a period of twenty years. It was about 1900, however, that this Electric Railway Company actually began service in Marion, according to record there, when its first cars hauled coal miners to Spillertown, north of Marion. But as coal development moved westward in Williamson County, the trolley line grew until it went to Peabody Mine No. 3, then "Fordville," Carterville and Herrin. The railroad reached Herrin before the town was built up, and therefore the main street, Park Avenue, was made wide enough to accomodate it. By 1902, there were numerous deep-shaft mines quite near these towns, and the hundreds of coal miners needed rail transportation to get to and from work. The automobile was practically "as scarce as the proverbial hen's teeth" in those days!

Merta McNeil Sonner, daughter of the co-founder of Carterville, has related to the writer that about this time she was working in the Carterville Post Office, situated in Hampton Drug Store. H. W. Cann was postmaster then. When the last rails were laid at the end of the Herrin line and the street car was brought to Carterville for its initial run, she and Nora Hampton (who clerked in Hampton's, which was located then on the corner of East Illinois and South Division, the Carterville terminus) were given the first ride on the completed line, the contractors having promised these two popular young ladies the first ride.

The motorman, Gus Crain, known as "Jersey," was related to her by marriage, as was also the conductor, M. D. "Daugherty" Allen, who was married to her cousin, Dolly Walker. The Allens had a beautiful, little, brown-eyed, curly-haired daughter, not yet school age, and they resided in a two-story house at the corner of East Illinois and Walnut Streets, where the Masonic Temple now stands. Minta is now Mrs. A. W. Rogers, residing in West Frankfort. Every afternoon Minta's mother would put her on the car to ride in order "to get her out of the way"; but it was to the delight of her father.

Soon there were numerous passengers boarding or unloading from the novel car at Hampton's Drug Store, later the location of Joe Kelley's Drug Store, and across from the J. V. Walker clothing store. After the death of druggist Kelley, his wife, Grace, operated a popular confectionery on

111

this busy corner. It was a new and exciting convenience to the townspeople to go on the trolley to visit relatives or friends in Herrin or Marion or way-stops in between, and get to return to Carterville all in the same day. Too, it was considered fashionable to go shopping in those two progressive towns, "where the grass seemed greener." It gave one almost the important feeling of going via Illinois Central Railroad to "far-off" St. Louis to shop. Which also brings to mind how difficult it was for the up-to-date, well-dressed ladies of our town to board the street car when wearing the ankle-length, very narrow skirts in vogue in 1914, when walking was all but impossible—let alone trying to get into the trolley car, with its exceedingly high step. Forrest Hampton recalls that once a prominent lady trying to step up into the car couldn't make it, and "Jersey" Crain lost patience in waiting for her, so he just picked her up bodily and set her on her feet firmly inside the car.

The most popular waiting place was the spacious dry goods department of the Elles Store just "kitty cornered" across Division Street from the Kelley corner. Elles Store had a large corner entrance under its pretentious cupola, with long glass double doors. Just inside on the right were a number of revolving stools so comfortable to sit upon, as well as good vantage-places while gazing out to watch the incoming car. In 1906 the Hampton Drug Store, the former place, had moved to its present location.

A short spur track led from the main line to the freight car depot. The depot was constructed by putting two boxcars together, one used as a depository for freight, and the other made into a very commodious office. It stood facing west on Pennsylvania Avenue, across from which was the printing shop where L. E. Robertson, an early editor of the *Carterville Herald*, published this weekly newspaper.

The Christian Science Church now occupies the first location of the *Herald*. Harvey Crain, still a resident here and a subscriber to the *Herald,* was the first freight agent from 1912-1916, then left the Coal Belt Line to go into train service. Mary Harriss succeeded him, working two years, followed by Elta Mangum, who had just finished Brown's Business College in Marion. Miss Mangum later married Frank Burns, a motorman on the line. Mr. Burns' brother, George, worked for several years also as a Coal Belt conductor.

The Coal Belt Railway Company was later bought by the Missouri Pacific Railroad, but in the early days was known as the Iron Mountain Railroad. Mrs. Burns continued to work for the company, and after forty-five years of freight service she was retired and now lives in Johnston City, Illinois. I am indebted to both Harvey Crain and Elta Burns for much of the first-hand information they have given me concerning the enormous amount and kinds of freight that was handled to and from this freight center here.

A regulation governing freight traffic had been stipulated at the onset by a city ordinance in 1902: "In no case shall the company haul through the streets of Carterville trains exceeding four cars in length, and through freight cars shall be hauled between the hours of 6 p.m. and 7 a.m., at no time shall car or cars be allowed to remain standing in any part of said Avenue (Illinois)."

Thus a great amount of freight hauling had been anticipated, and the city fathers had planned wisely for it to be transported during the nocturnal hours so as not to impede the daytime passenger service. Mrs. Burns has stated that this traffic regulation was not always strictly adhered to, for oftentimes the demand was so heavy that boxcars and loaded, long flatcars were pulled in or out the depot during daylight hours especially to accommodate waiting farmers who had driven into town by wagons and teams from their farms south and west of Carterville to obtain the lime-dust shipped from the large quarry at Menard, near Chester. Harvey Crain has stated, too, that it was only in the later years of the company's operation here that the lime-dust became available as a fertilizer for farming in this area. Mr. Crain has recalled also that, in the shipment of sand, cement and lime-rock, all were to be used by the Johnson Flodine Construction Company for the building of the then-first narrow slab pavement south of Carterville, one and one-fourth or one and one-half miles to Crab Orchard Creek, part of which is submerged now by the Crab Orchard Lake. The loaded cars were pulled to the end of the rails on Illinois Avenue to Division Street at the town square, there to be conveyed onto the company trucks. The big, red caboose-like freight car known as Electric Car Number One was used for this purpose, the reason being that steam engines were not allowed on the track.

In speaking of local freight, Mrs. Burns has revealed some interesting sidelights. Bags of beans, sugar and coffee as well as barrels of sorghum molasses and stalks of bananas were shipped here after being unloaded from boxcars from St. Louis via the Iron Mountain Railroad at the Herrin depot yard, then transferred to Electric Car Number One to be taken to Marion or to be brought on to Carterville. On reaching the freight depot here these commodities were then "drayed" by the well-known drayman, Bennie Smith, to the Arch Howell and W. V. Craig Grocery Stores on South Division Street, located where Teen Town now is. In regard to bananas, one could buy a whole stalk for fifty cents.

Mrs. Burns related an interesting story of a man who got into the banana compartment, reached in to grab some and lost his valuable ring. It was finally discovered by the merchant here to whom the bananas had been delivered. She also tells of Mon Colp, of the Colp-Arnold Flouring Mill here, shipping through her office many twenty-four pound bags of flour and ten-pound bags of corn meal at a charge of fifty cents per hundred pounds, to be delivered off the line at Hafer Crossing, Taylor Crossing, or Energy en route to Herrin, or perhaps to Crenshaw Crossing or Peabody No. Three Crossing, known as the Electric Park, enroute to Marion.

As to passenger service, Mrs. Burns has stated that she sold tickets at her office for awhile but people didn't like to walk to the freight depot from downtown, two blocks away, when the car stopped to take on passengers, so tickets

114

were then obtained at the Will Allen Chevrolet Auto Agency in the Modern Woodmen of America Building at the corner of Walnut Street and Illinois, which now houses the Tregoning Antique Store. Later the ticket office was moved two doors west in the J. J. Hunter Building where Helen Harris, now Helen Peach, collected the gas bills there. Helen had just finished her Brown's Business College Course having graduated from Carterville High School that same year, 1917, and had commuted on the trolley line daily to Brown's at Marion. Prices of tickets as nearly as she can remember were ten cents to Energy, fifteen cents to Herrin and twenty-five cents to Marion. Helen enjoyed selling car fares. However, her big problem was making out the intricate monthly reports, and she affirms that without Elta's help she could not have done it. She remembers there were long wooden benches in her office for waiting passengers.

Schoolchildren in this district could ride into town to attend school and return for ten cents a round trip. Bertha and Nellie McNeil, residing just beyond the city limits east at McNeil crossing, and Myrtle Mason, later Mrs. Liston Carey, from Hafer Crossing, were regular passengers throughout their grade and high-school days here. After Bertha's graduation (she was the only graduate that year, 1911) she went to work at Baker Ghent Department Store as cashier and bookkeeper.

With convenient transportation by the electric cars now available to everyone, a tremendous business had developed. Passengers were being forced to stand, and by 1918 there were not enough cars to carry the customers. Not only were miners packed into the cars for the early morning and late afternoon trips to and from their work, but business people and shoppers traveling between the cities on the line had difficulty in finding seats. There was no restriction either on miners riding the cars in their grimy, greasy, black, pit clothes. However, that was no fault of theirs; for in the early days of coal mining in this area there were no wash-houses at the mines. Consequently the workmen had to wear

115

their work clothes home, where usually they had their own wash-houses heated by laundry stoves or coal ranges, and zinc washtubs for bathing— no city water, only cistern and well-water available.

A memorable Easter Sunday I recall, I think it was in 1913, I was invited home from church with the McNeil sisters. I did not wear "a sweet little Alice blue gown" that day, but I felt very dressed up in my brand-new, pretty, nile-green, wool batiste frock with wide bands of ecru lace trimming. It could have been a 1969 creation—so similar in style now. It was made especially for me by a prominent local dressmaker. When we reached the McNeil home we discovered I had sat on a long greasy spot—pit clothes the factor, no doubt— and the skirt was ruined. There were no cleaning shops then and talcum powder would not remove it.

It was several years later, in fact, on October 5, 1920, that the city council passed an ordinance which stated, "Whoever shall spit or expertorate upon any sidewalk, or upon the floor or steps of any public building, street car, passenger coach or other public conveyance within the city, shall be fined not less than one dollar nor more than ten dollars." I feel sure this ordinance was not always abided by in Carterville's trolley-car days, but I do know those were the days of spittoons, and I find no record of fines imposed for dirty car seats.

One employee who spent ten years as motorman and conductor has stated, "I've seen the cars so crowded that we would have to pull away from the station and leave some of the people behind. We hauled a lot of people between towns for special events such as basketball games and lodge meetings. Sometimes a group could charter a car for twenty-five dollars." The writer recalls that it was in July, 1910 that all the eighth-grade graduates of Carterville School District 35, and the eighth-grade graduates from several one-room rural schools across Crab Orchard and Grassy Creeks, went to Marion by street car to participate in our county commencement program, held in the historic Roland theater there.

The old, red Electric Car Number One had been chartered to bring those who lived in Herrin and Carterville back, since it was after 11 p.m., the last run of the "owl" car. But we really felt important and had so much fun riding on the long wooden side benches in that big freight car. In the latter years of its era it was pressed into service each September to bring back to Carterville many passengers who had attended either of the two big days, Thursday or Friday, of the noted Williamson County Fair. The Illinois Central Railroad coaches, often twelve to fourteen attached to the steam locomotive, were inadequate to transport all the people on the return trip—the last train incoming from Marion around 7 p.m., and even standing room at a premium.

There is more to be mentioned of life around the freight depot. Sina McCabe happily remembers that a favorite pastime of the children in that neighborhood was placing a series of pins on the car tracks, and after the car went by to run out and pick up the pins which had been flattened into miniature "scissors."

In preparation of laying the tracks for the Coal Belt Railway, the long, sloping, high hill on East Illinois known as Pea Ridge was cut down on both sides of the right of way. It was quite a deep cut as it neared the apex of the Ridge. I recall that only the upper part of the porches and rooftops could be seen as the street car joltingly swayed, clanging and rattling along. The interior of the car had comfortable reversible seats covered with a kind of basket-weave straw matting.

At this point it is timely to muse on Maxine Moore Walker's memories, as related to me, of her childhood while living at the top of Pea Ridge. The deep cut was most attractive to both the boys and girls, who would slide down the steep yellow clay embankment in the manner of a "ski run," using old pieces of tin, boards, and sometimes dishpans to toboggan down to the railway track. Great sport it was!

Many children resided along the Avenue cut on both sides, and as the motorman on the old car continuously clanged the bell before rounding the sweeping curve from McNeil

117

crossing as it entered the Avenue to come into town, the kids would all come flocking to the edge of the cut to see the trolley pass. At night they were hilarious with glee as they watched for the car's big headlight that indicated its approach, and the sparks from the high trolley wire giving notice it would soon pass their homes.

The adventuresome boys would sometimes get on the tracks, which worried their mothers not a little.

Maxine further remembers that her youngest brother, not yet school age, did this one time. Her mother kept hearing the clanging of the bell, and hastening down into the cut, seeing her little son calmly lying there, she promptly reprimanded him, to which he replied. "Why, don't you know 'Jersey' would not run over me!" Sure enough, the kind motorman had brought the car to a halt just in time.

She also recalls the high concrete retaining wall the company had constructed on the south side of the cut. It was probably ten to twelve inches thick, making a fine walkway the children enjoyed going back and forth—on one foot at a time inching along, but all the while in playful, exuberant laughter.

At Halloween the larger boys and girls in the neighborhood thought it great sport to soap the tracks. They also placed pins on the tracks to see what fantastic flattened shapes would result, which provided them such fascinating "metal jewelry."

On one Halloween occasion three young boys in their late teens, all of them from prominent families, smeared a lot of soap on the tracks on Pea Ridge hill; and when the next car came along it gained so much momentum that the motorman was unable to stop it when it reached the end of the tracks at Joe Kelley's Drug Store. Consequently, it jumped its terminal point and slid across Division Street, not stopping until it was between Elles Store and the Carterville State and Savings Bank on West Illinois Avenue. This story is attested by Frank Samuel, Sr. and Raymond Talley; however, neither of them were among the culprits. But Raymond affirms that one of them who is still living feared for many years he would get arrested for participating in this prank, and never revealed his guilt until long after he was an adult.

Then, too, how they did enjoy picking up off the tracks bits of welded metal, a golden hue that had been slivered off the steel spikes—and they imagined these were actual gold! All in all, these street-car-line children created their own amusement and games when this electric railway was literally at their door steps.

What greater joy could they ask for in those days, with the trolley car passing back and forth every hour? How they loved to get on the car at Kelley's Drug Store after school, when it was so crowded with passengers, and ride as far as Pea Ridge Crossing, while the car hadn't picked up full speed and the conductor was kept so busy taking up the regular tickets he was unaware there were several schoolchildren riding in the rear entrance. Then, when the motorman stopped at that crossing, the children would scamper down the car step happy that they had had a free ride to Pea Ridge. "Yes," Maxine says, "those were the days!"

In a more serious mood, Maxine Walker has related to the writer the names of other crossings in the neighborhood where, if one missed Pea Ridge, by running, the car could be beaten before it gained momentum either at Carter Crossing or Hampton.

Beyond the latter, after passing McNeil there was a long trestle which the kids fearfully walked on Sunday afternoon, between hours of the approaching car. Hafer Crossing was more often known as "Punkin," the nickname of the nearby Hafer mine were many miners worked.

There was also Taylor Crossing between Energy and Herrin which accommodated numerous miners who worked at the Taylor One and Two Mines. Then going towards Marion was Crenshaw Crossing, and nearing the county seat, Peabody Number Three.

At this crossing was Electric Park, a popular amusement and recreational place. Dances were often held there; and

Mrs. Logan (Laura) Colp has laughingly told how she one time slipped off from home to attend a dance there, to the chagrin of her father. Nearby was the noted three-room village school known as LaMaster, which boasted a very high professional caliber of teachers. Opal Crain, sister of Fay Skinner, taught there with Hazel Peterson of Ferges and Lou Doerr of Marion.

I must mention the year of the deep snow, 1917. I remember it well. The blizzard lasted half a day and a night. Business places and home owners got busy the next morning to dig paths along the sidewalks in town. These were practically tunnels between walls some thirty to thirty-six inches high.

Helen Peach tells how this heavy snow affected the car-line. She was going to Brown's Business College, and a street car would be sent from Energy to meet the eastbound Carterville car halfway. Passengers would transfer to the Energy car. In like manner another car, northbound from Marion, would be sent halfway to Energy to take on the passengers off the Energy car—and thus she and the Marion-bound passengers would finally reach Marion.

It was the coming of the paved roads that killed the Coal Belt Electric Railway. By 1926 the company was asking the state for permission to discontinue passenger service because of the lack of patronage. This came about due to the automobile and the roads that had been built for it to travel. The miners were buying automobiles. Car pools among them were organized. Bus transportation was available. Faster service was assured the workers, as they didn't have to await the inter-urban's hourly departures. The paved roads were a boon.

At midnight on November 15, 1926, the last car made its final run. The Missouri Pacific Railroad bought the line, the facilities of which were valued at $513.58.

So ends the street-car era in this noted Coal Belt area that spanned almost the entire first quarter of this 20th century. After the tracks were taken up and the company refilled the deep cut, it was many years before Illinois Avenue could be hard-surfaced, for the ground sank so much due to the freezing and thawing during the hard winter, plus the heavy spring rains prevalent in this climate.

However with the big fill-in the street was made very wide. Driving up along Pea Ridge today, a wonderful view to the east can be seen; and the many nice homes with their bordering trees, especially the numerous red buds, are a glory to enjoy in the springtime.

Old Streetcar in Carterville
On the cars of the Coal Belt Electric Railway the conductor was M. D. Allen, and the motorman was Gus Crain.

CHAPTER VII

THE THREE "MOTHER" STORES OF CARTERVILLE

Carterville has now entered its centennial year, 1971. At this point it is timely to relate other specific history of the three "mother" stores that originated here after the founding of the village of Carterville, and branched out into other towns in Williamson County as well as additional offsprings in other Illinois counties. Then, too, one of them in particular established stores in the State of Ohio.

To begin at the beginning, the Carbondale and Shawneetown Railroad as it was being constructed, sought permission to cross George M. McNeill's forty-acre farm, and wanted to build a depot on it. The rairoad men told him they would place it anywhere he wished it. A depot situated at a convenient spot near the post office was definitely needed, not only to handle the shipment of railroad supplies and lumber for the budding village, but also the coal to be transported from the Laban Carter farm a mere half-mile east of the McNeill homestead—as well as a port of entry (so to speak) for people of note connected with the coal and railroad business, or the curious-minded business prospectors of whom Albert K. Elles and brother Edward A. Elles are the most noteworthy. These two youthful brothers from Belleville envisioned a merchantile establishment and, being regular boarders at the McNeill Hotel, were in first-hand position to purchase a choice location at the northwest corner of Division Street and Illinois Avenue, laying the foundation for their business enterprise in 1875 known as Elles Store. Mr. McNeill had had his forty acres surveyed and platted, naming the streets himself. The depot had been built where

Olive Street, named after Mr. McNeill's first wife, joined West Illinois Avenue at the railroad crossing. I have been told by Mrs. Sonner that Edward A. Elles was only fifteen years old when he and his brother Albert took up board at her father's hotel. By 1877 these enterprising young men had erected a small frame building 20 x 40 feet which was their first store venture.

In 1891, the co-partnership known as Elles Store Company was formed by the addition of two other Elles brothers, also from Belleville, namely Louis and Charles. Two years later this company erected a large brick building facing North Division Street. The date 1891 was in prominent view at the top. This impressive building with its peaked cupola above the corner entrance was an outstanding landmark on the street for many years until the cupola was removed due to the modern improvement of Heckels, Inc., which still occupies much of the original space, practically a block, except the part on the corner, now rented to Midtown Grocery. Incidentally A. G. Heckel, nephew of the Elles brothers, who now heads this corporation, came to Carterville around 1916 or 1917 to serve as credit manager in Elles Store Company.

The business was built primarily upon the solid foundation of merit. A photograph published in 1905 shows the new brick building with its twenty-six employees standing in front under a large striped awning spread all across, bearing these words: "ELLES STORE CO. MAKERS OF UNIFORMLY LOW PRICES." Which reminds me of a true incident told to me recently by a Carterville native lady from her early childhood memories. It goes like this: A group of children were playing hide-and-seek around the barn just back of the store, where Heckels' and Midtown Grocery parking lot is now, and they spied a barrel of tar. Each took a piece and was chewing on it. Louis Elles saw them and called them into the grocery department, having them deposit the wads of tar on the counter. He proceeded to give them a lecture in a kind way on honesty, showing them that taking little things leads to larger thefts—an object-lesson, she says, they never forgot.

In the book entitled Williamson County, Illinois in World War 1917-1918, published by Hal W. Trovillion in 1919, it states: "The rules of the corporation as well as the early organization was to give everyone a square deal and thereby merit the confidence of the people of Williamson County, and its management will always stand for the square deal for the young, the old, the rich and the poor alike." This record also distinquishes Elles Store Company as Williamson County's largest merchantile establishment.

I was a salesgirl in the large dry-goods and ready-to-wear department of this store from 1915 to 1919, it being my first public job when I was fresh out of high school. I remember vividly the great rolls of wrapping paper, as were used in those days in each department, which always bore the slogan in bold black letters: "MERIT." Thus I became conscious of this, the firm's solid business creed. Incidentally, the large painted sign on the south wall facing West Illinois Avenue can still be distinguished in bold yellow letters, but now dimmed with the years.

In scanning over old records showing pictures of the numerous stores that emerged from the "mother" store, I have noted the following:

The Herrin branch opened in 1897 and later became known as the Herrin Supply Company.

The Lauder branch was opened in 1900 under the name Elles Store Company. This branch was later known as the store at Reeves and still later the Cambria Store. The village of Cambria has borne three names, which is most unique as well as significant in our neighboring village's history. Some years ago Jettie Vaughn purchased this store and operated it many years. But somewhat recently sold it to a man by the name of Griffith.

The Marion branch of Elles Store Company came into existence in 1901. It was first located on the east side of the public square at the southeast corner of East Main Street.

The upper story was occupied by the New Goodall Hotel. Eli D. Roach was general manager of this branch. Mr. Roach at the time resided in Carterville. His home, still standing, is just opposite the old flouring mill, until recently a landmark in our town.

Another branch soon afterwards was opened at Whiteash just north of Spillertown to serve that mining area near Johnston City, Illinois.

Referring again to Hal Trovillion's book, published in 1919, there is a fine picture showing the impressive two-story brick building with the large, white letters, "Marion Supply Company," across the front, this building on the north side of East Main Street opposite the present Post Office. Under the picture are these words: "BUILT TO ACCOMMODATE THE GROWING BUSINESS IN OUR COUNTY SEAT." I remember this store well, and no doubt older residents do too. I do not know the volume of business at that time, but I find the record shows the Herrin Supply Company supplied the citizens of the county with nearly three-quarter of a million dollar's worth of merchandise in 1918 at a uniformly low price considering the prevailing high prices; and it adds, "We sell everything under the sun. If you are in Herrin, Murphysboro, Carbondale, Hillsboro, West Frankfort, Eldorado or Benton, ask for Herrin Supply Company stores. Trade at them and you will come out ahead. Don't fail to read about Elles Store Company and Marion Supply Company in this book. We are kin." We now know that these various branches from the "mother" trunk in Carterville had extended into Franklin, Jackson, and Saline Counties and had reached up north as far as Montgomery County at Hillsboro, the county seat there.

In my childhood I remember Miss Ella Roach, who was the buyer in the dry-goods department of the mother store, and of her transfer to the Hillsboro store where she worked a number of years. She was a shrewd businesswoman, a sister to her equally shrewd brother, Elli D. Roach. Mr. Roach had changed his residence from Carterville to Marion prior

125

to my employment in the Carterville store, but he also was credit manager for the original store.

The street-car line was in its heyday then, so transportation on the Coal Belt Interurban electric cars with hourly service between these two towns was expedient for his weekly visits to check accounts.

One morning "Mr. Ed" as the many employees respectfully addressed Edward A. Elles, entered the front corner entrance —there was another front entrance— punched the big time-clock and was hurrying through the dry-goods department as I was dusting one of the large showcases. He stopped abruptly and said, "Miss Cavanas, I have designs on you," and beckoned me to follow him to the office. I didn't know what he meant, but I immediately acquiesced, although with qualms. As we entered the large office in the back part of the store I saw Mr. Roach sitting at a desk and the several office girls busy at theirs. Mr. Ed then explained that the credit manager needed help to check the numerous charge sales slips, some of which were scribbled so badly they resembled chicken tracks. Mr. Roach put me at ease immediately, and as I deciphered those semihieroglyphic pencil-scratchings he remarked, "You are my hawk-eyes, for many of these I cannot read." After that Mr. Ed had me work with Mr. Roach at this kind of task a number of times.

There were other outstanding men and women who got their business training in merchandising as employees of Elles Store Company. Notable was G. W. Bevard, brother-in-law to Mr. Ed. In 1905 Mr. Bevard had already worked some thirteen years for the firm first as an outside salesman, then a house salesman, and five years as collector and judge of credits. He left this employment a few years later and established a store of his own just across the street. remaining in his own successful business until his death.

Another outstanding employee was Arthur Baker, who had been with the company twelve years, seven of which serving as secretary. In 1901 Mr. Baker with several of his relatives and his brother-in-law, Walter Ghent, organized and established a large general merchantile business on Division Street just a block south from Elles Store. It was so successful that in a few years Baker-Ghent's had set up another store in Marion, its location in the 1920's on West Main Street. The Carterville Store occupied the space of the present Bay's Foodland.

As early as 1882 an Englishman named H. W. Cann became associated with Elles Store Company, working for it also twelve years, after which he was mayor of the town and also served as postmaster. While postmaster he had the distinction of recommending the issue of the thirteen-cent stamp and getting Carterville as the first fourth-class post office to issue foreign money orders through his persistency. He is accredited also in naming the small village about a mile north of Carterville "Dewmaine" in 1898, reminiscent of the Spanish-American War. It is significant to note that the citizens of Dewmaine who were mostly Negroes were regular customers of Elles Store Company, Bevards, and Baker-Ghent Stores. On mine paydays, especially those of Madison, Colp, Donaly, and Burr mines, the stores kept open late hours to accommodate the scores of these people including the foreign laborers with others who came into town "to trade," as it was called then instead of the modern term "shopping." I especially remember a regular customer, Dr. Birdie McLean Springs, the wife of the prominent Negro-Indian doctor, A. W. Springs of Dewmaine. She carried her own charge account in her name where I clerked, and her name was listed in the stores "Good-book" of dependable accredited customers.

C. E. Anderson, son-in-law to Dr. Perry, one of Carterville's early doctors, entered into the service of Elles Store Company in 1901, and through his aptitude in the management of its interest became Director and Manager of the Herrin branch.

Both Robert Hopper and J. G. Applegath are equally noteworthy to mention in the significant roles they served. The former was assistant manager of the branch store at Herrin;

the latter, manager at whiteash. There are others that could be mentioned that had responsible positions credited by the now-recognized, historically famous Elles Brothers.

Now I must mention briefly the second important "mother" store that originated in Carterville, founded in 1884 by J. V. Walker, at the northeast corner of Carterville's village square, and incidentally directly opposite Elles Store. In Chapter I is its detailed story.

Also, I must mention the third "mother" store that originated in Carterville in 1903 when Snyder S. Vick set up a most modern and complete drug store in a fine two-story brick building situated on South Division Street. When he moved to Johnston City in 1918, where he had purchased a drug store, this was the first branch of the parent store. There in a very short while S. S. Vick became most popular, and was usually known as "Snyder" by his many friends in Williamson County. That same year, 1918, he became a partner in the Cline-Vick Drug Store in Zeigler. In the Johnston City store a music room was located in the rear where sheet music and musical instruments were sold, such as Victor talking machines, latest records, Adam Schaaf and Vose pianos and players. These stores became known as the Rexall stores, which by this time was a household word throughout both Williamson and Franklin Counties. The firm was then known as the Cline-Vick Drug Company. By the early 1920's the company had established other stores in Carbondale, Marion and West Frankfort. Mr. Vick's partner, Leo V. Cline, had opened his own drug store in Herrin in 1904. With these two aggressive and progressive druggists pooling joint resources and know-how in management, the name Cline-Vick became noted all over Southern Illinois as far north as Salem in Marion County.

Much more could be written about these three "mother" stores which stemmed from Carterville's early grass roots; but the important thing is that each has left a heritage of service to the people based on a vision of progress for the upbuilding of the comunities wherever they transplanted a root. We cannot deny that these early store founders have meant much to the economic status over a broad area, Williamson County in particular.

This recorded research has been my memorial to them.

Burr "C" Mine Tipple and Miners, 1904
Front row (in white) George Lockie, young hoisting engineer; Frank Bevard, mine superintendent is eighth from left in back row.

CHAPTER VIII

ABOUT MINING IN CARTERVILLE AND EARLY INDUSTRIES

Closely related with the history of the coming of the railroad to Carterville, there were many notable miners who rose from working in the pits with pick and shovel to positions of authority relating to mines, and who had much to do with advancement of mining in this area. According to record, I now mention some of them that are of outstanding note.

Alexander Lauder, a native of Scotland, located here in 1872. He was elected one of the village trustees, served several terms, then elected treasurer in 1877. At the time he took charge of the Carterville Coal and Coke Company's property it was the only shipping mine in Williamson County. By 1905 the county had over forty coal openings. Mr. Lauder had seen the great coal industry of Williamson County grow from the little slope on the Laban Carter estate to one of the most noted coal fields of America. He died October 9, 1904. His two sons, James A. and Frank, reached prominence in the city's history also. The former, born in 1869, was brought with his parents to Carterville when a child and the record reads: "The country at that time was mostly a wilderness and the family had all the hardships and privations of pioneer life. James A. went to mining where he worked till about twenty years old. In 1898 he was appointed Postmaster, which office he held many years." The record further states it was the first office in the county to secure Rural Free Delivery with the following carriers (as of July 1, 1905): Richard Stover, Route 1; John W. Hestand, Route 2; Roscoe

North, Route 3; Miss Pearl Robinson, Assistant Postmaster; Anna McCutcheon, clerk. The office was a distributing center for the surrounding towns, handling the Blairsville, North Bend and Clifford mails, about half of Dewmaine and Fordville, and more than a fourth of Herrin in transit.

The other son, Frank, also worked as a miner, first at Madison No. 8, then at Madison No. 9, advancing to mine manager over the latter, serving in this administrative position a number of years.

Walter Tregoning left his native country of Scotland in 1869 after much experience working in iron and coal mines and also three years sinking shafts. In 1880 he came to Carterville, after following mining at Caseyville and Murphysboro. He was foreman of the Dodd shaft. In 1884 he was made superintendent of the Dodd mine. He was also superintendent of a mine and coke ovens in Jackson County. It was while he was at Old Dodd that he taught his nine-year-old son, Charles B. Tregoning to run the engine; and he would get a box for the little lad to stand on so he could reach the throttle. There were no child-labor laws then. On growing up Charles B. became a notable hoisting engineer at the Old Burr mine, and after that mine was worked out he was transferred to the new shaft, "Burr C," where he remained as one of the three hoisting engineers working in shifts with George Lockie and Walter Hadfield until that mine, too, closed down. All in all, Mr. Tregoning had a fifty-year record as a hoisting engineer. His daughter, Mrs. Mae Bleyer, who has given me this information, has also stated that her father was a charter member of the United Mine Workers of America of the State of Illinois long before the various local unions were organized. Walter Tregoning had another son, George, who became a prominent miner and during the Depression sank and operated his own mine.

William Lockie, another Scotchman, coming from his native town of Kelso in 1880, was also a hoisting engineer for Old Dodd and then went to new Burr C, which had the best coal anywhere; and it was a nine-foot-thick vein. But

131

when Mr. Lockie was ill, his son George, then at an early age, became a hoisting engineer. In an interview with George Lockie a few years ago, he said he was born on July 12, 1882 in a log cabin near a little creek that ran through what was then called the Prentice Farm, now the site of the Carterville Community High School. Prentice Street borders these grounds today. Mr. Lockie went on to say that as a young lad he, with Snyder S. Vick, often drove Dr. Vick's cow and other cows to pasture there. He told the writer also that he was proud of the fact that he had helped sink the Burr C mine with my father and other laborers around 1901 or 1902, and was hoisting engineer there until that mine, too, was worked out and closed down sometime in the 1920's.

An early photograph shows George Lockie and many miners with their pit-caps and attached pit-lamps on and holding their big tin "dinner buckets," seated near the shaft entrance, with its towering black tipple. This picture apparently was taken right after they had been hoisted on the cage to the surface. In the group Frank C. Bevard, mine manager, is clearly distinguishable, wearing his familiar broad-brimmed felt mine-hat. No doubt Mr. Will Thompson, mine superintendent, is in this group, too.

Another prominent man of Scotch descent, James R. Watson, known as "Jimsie" and father of the late Irene Watson, was one of Burr's mine examiners. I remember him as a prominent figure passing my girlhood home each mine working day. It was a familiar sight to see the miners from all parts of town walking to and from Burr C, regardless of the weather, a bare three-fourths of a mile from the northwest section of town.

It was early in the 1930's that the Pregenser Coal Company of near Antioch, Illinois acquired rights from the Peabody Coal Company, who held ninety-nine-year leases on the coal underlying the W. E. Sizemore farm and the adjoining Phillips land, for permission to "strip" this large acreage to "pull the pillars" of coal left from the underground workings of Burr C. Accordingly the Pregenser Company brought in their steam shovel and drag-line equipment with some skilled machine operators. Some local miners were hired. It was entirely something new in this area. I remember that after the "stripping" I walked with my brother over to the edge of the huge, deep pit (just a short distance from my home to view this awesome chasm), and my brother pointing out to me the unusually thick, eleven-foot vein of coal, revealing some of the rooms and entries with the pillars in which he and my father had worked underground years before, and explaining that the pillars would soon be broken up and shipped away. Later the Forsythe Coal Company replaced the Pregenser and obtained rights to strip the Sizemore acreage on the east side of the hard road near the Sycamore Crossroads. The ugly strip-hills or strip-piles, as they are now called, were the unsightly result to become filled with mine water that is a pollution problem today. What a pity legislation was not enacted during those Depression years as it is today to make it mandatory that the scarred lands be filled and levelled so the farms could be productive again. Other farmlands all around met a similar fate during those hard years.

Since the safety lamp was for many years not accepted into the mine, it was David Wallace, grandfather of Gilbert D. Wallace, who in America first introduced the canary into the mines to check for gas. Mr. Wallace was also a native of Scotland and at one time was mine inspector for Williamson County, and was also Superintendent of Mine Safety in Illinois. It is said that a noted folklore singer of today would come on many a Sunday and sit for hours on David Wallace's front porch at 118 Virginia Avenue, and Mr. Wallace would teach him words and tunes of American and Scottish songs. These sessions his wife (Amanda, the "Duchess") detested, closing the windows and doors to avoid hearing the music—she called it noise. One hot day, she had had enough, so she went to the well and drew a huge bucket of water. Opening the front door, she doused them both with the chilling water; and it did end the sessions for several weeks.

133

Another most interesting story Gilbert has sent to me is as follows:

I am reminded of a famous and rather unusual guest that Carterville had around 1914 or 1915. He arrived in Carbondale (I think) and thence to Carterville by coach, probably from an engagement in Chicago. From what I have been able to find out, he slipped into Carterville without fanfare and for the most part without the knowledge of its citizens. He visited with my grandfather, David Wallace, at 118 Virginia Avenue. It was the great Harry Lauder, who was born in Portobellow, Scotland on August 4, 1870. Grandfather had tutored him when he first entered the Hamilton Mines as a "pit-boy," and he was always grateful to him. It was long after my grandfather left Scotland that Harry Lauder presented himself to the Gatti's Music Hall in London and entered show business. The year was 1900. Lauder was such a success that he was booked for three hundred consecutive weeks. He made numerous trips to America while on tour. Each tour was a success, but he felt somehow or other that each would be his last; and so they were acclaimed "farewell tours." It was in 1914 that he made his seventh "farewell tour," and there were countless others after that date.

Lauder's usual week in America brought him $3,000.00 to $4,000.00 each. He insisted on being paid at least in two or three $1,000.00 bills and at least one $500.00 bill, the balance in small currency. When asked why so much in small bills, he would always retort, "For ma piggy bank."

Due to transportation in those days, Lauder was sometimes late in arrival; and it is known that his audience had waited for him as long as four hours, and still greeted him with an ovation. His opening remark in such a situation was usually, "Ha ye na hame?"

It has been said that the most exuberant record ever recorded was made the first day of November 1926 and was called "Soosie MacLean." His best-remembered, however, was "Roamin' in the Gloamin'," recorded in Europe of the same

134

year, and a "Wee Dooch an' Doris," recorded the second day of November, 1926.

Sir Harry didn't want publicity at Carterville, for it would only cut down on his visitation time. However, when Alex Hutton dropped in to visit my grandfather that day and met the great Sir Harry, he never forgot it and sometimes would say, "Shake the hand which shook the hand of the famous Sir Harry Lauder."

Which brings to mind that it was about 1895 when Alex Hutton, another native Scotchman, with his wife and children came from Murphysboro by train and was met at the depot here by my father with a springboard wagon and team of horses, and they were taken direct to the Scoby home on my grandfather's (W. E. Sizemore's) farm at the Sycamore Cross-roads just a mile north. There they boarded for a while until Mr. Hutton could rent or buy a house. He and his sixteen-year-old son, Jim, were experienced miners; and my mother enjoyed telling of how young Jim, on returning from his day's work at the Old Burr (not far distant near the Burr Woods) would pick me up as I lay crying in my cradle to hush me while she was preparing supper.

In those days boys were taken into the mines to work with their fathers. Wages were small, however. Some boys got jobs as "trappers" or "trip-riders." Mules were used to pull the loaded pit-cars to the "cage" to be hoisted and return the "empties" to the entries and rooms, to be filled again by the hard-working miners.

A clipping in my possession from an old *Carterville Herald* dated April 1, 1948 is of timely interest at this junction in my story. At the top of the printed item are reproductions of two pictures of the Old Burr mine provided by Sam Murphy, son of John Murphy, owner of one of the early Carterville livery stables. In 1894, Sam's father began feeding and caring for the "pit mules" for the Carterville Coal Company, which he continued to do until 1903. (Some of the mules are shown in the picture.) The published item reads: "Fifty years ago on April 1, 1898 the coal miners of Southern

Illinois celebrated the beginning of a new era—a changeover from the ten-hour working day to a new eight-hour day which has been in effect ever since, except for the nine-hour shifts worked during the war. At the Old Burr mine northeast of Carterville coal miners worked ten hours a day. For many years that was the last day following the change, Southern Illinois miners traditionally celebrated April 1st as a holiday denoting their victory in the fight for the eight-hour day. These pictures, taken fifty years ago—March 31, 1898—at the Old Burr Mine, were provided by Sam Murphy of Ferges. Murphy, a little boy then, is shown in the center of the lower picture. Murphy is still on a coal-mine payroll."

Not many weeks ago Sam Murphy telephoned me from his residence in Herrin and reminisced about his parents and their home here in Carterville in his childhood.

In the early 1900's it was not uncommon for miners to receive their wages or part of it in gold. I remember how thrilled our family was if my father found in his pay envelope a gold piece in a five, ten, or twenty-dollar denomination— the latter very rare. By 1926 miners averaged $50 to $60 for two weeks' work, sometimes $100.

But, looking back, I recall difficult times when mines were on strike. One in particular stands out when, in April, 1910, a strike was called which lasted six months. I was a freshman in high school beginning that fall, and when Burr C blew its long, shrill whistle on a September afternoon, Mr. L. L. Jones, our Latin teacher, was holding our class at that time. Tears of joy flowed down his cheeks as he unashamedly joined all of us in joyful tears—the merchants' children as well as those whose fathers were miners. Many other mine whistles in the area with their individual tones and whistling shrieks were likewise proclaiming the good news! But the whistles of the numerous mines at unpredictable times sounded weirdly five times in succession, indicating that a fatality, in or about the pit, had occurred, and that some wife would be widowed, perhaps, or children suddenly become fatherless.

136

This ominous boding was ever-present day or night in a miner's family.

Now, back to that day of joyful news! I recall the new life in the business section of town. Especially in Elles Store, activity reigned! Vida Brown and Jake Ford of the Dry Goods and Clothing Departments were following Mr. Ed's instruction to put on special sale, on a big table in the middle aisle, bolts and bolts of pretty calico (we would call it "prints" now) priced at 4¢ a yard! Miners' wives hastened to the sale to purchase materials for their children's dresses and boys' and men's shirts. My mother chose two patterns of the material, five yards each, which she would sew into new school dresses for me. She had made over my old dresses during the summer, even dying some of the materials to camouflage their age, so I was very happy at the prospect of owning two new school frocks.

More about the mine whistles, I must relate. Mrs. Edna Spires Travis was in the class of 1923, the last class to graduate from the old Carterville High School (the same building from which I graduated nine years before and in which Mr. Jones's Latin class was in session that joyful, memorable afternoon). She has said that she definitely remembers counting thirty-eight different mine whistles one morning as she was walking from home to the high school. Every whistle had a different tone and could easily be distinguished by a sharp and listening ear. Polluted air was not a subject of controversy then.

As the reader no doubt has already surmised, most of Carterville's early miners were Scotch people. There were some English and Welsh and others of German or Irish nationality. I recall only one Frenchman and a few Russian or Polish miners. The Frenchman was Alfred La Barr, whom the miners called "Frenchie." He and his Irish wife were nextdoor neighbors when my family moved to the Park Addition in the north part of town in 1902, when there were very few houses in that new section—just an alley dividing Park Addition and "John Town"—the alley called Pleasant, now marked as Pleasant Street and paved. I've been told by old residents in my childhood that the northwest section of town derived its name, "John Town," from the fact so many of its men occupants were named John. They were John Tippett, John Richardson, John Lewis, John Black, John Watson, John Burke, John Harris and others.

Now back to "Frenchie" LaBarr. I remember "Frenchie" launched out on a business venture when he bought a Merry-Go-Round or Carousel, as it is called today. He had it set up on a vacant lot near the railroad uptown—the lot on which later the Alexander Hotel was built—now the location of the bank's new drive-up facility. The Merry-Go-Round, however, was an unsuccessful business; and after its disposal he and Mrs. LaBarr and son, Tom, moved to California.

Mrs. LaBarr had a neice, Mrs. Frank (Mamie) Kenoskey, who lived across Quail Alley from us. The Kenoskeys had a boarder, a young man who went by the nickname "Russian Joe." He worked at the Prosperity mine just west of the city limits. The street on which they lived was named for that mine, that was owned by the Scott Wilson Mining Company. I remember the nice frame cottage in which they lived—it being unusual in that it had one single room jutting out of the roof upstairs, with windows on all four sides. This was "Russian Joe's" bedroom, and it was said the owner designed the home in keeping with Polish houses in his homeland, as Joe preferred also ventilation from all four directions. It was a sad day, however, when young miner Joe (who spoke very little English) was brought to his room badly burned from an explosion at the mine. He died shortly afterward. The pretty white and green cottage later burned. But before that, after Kenoskeys moved to East St. Louis, Dr. Aird with wife and small son Edgar lived in it a few months right after they came to Carterville to reside.

The greatest mine disaster not far from Carterville happened on January 10, 1962 at the Blue Blaze Mine, operated by Claude Gentry, when eleven miners lost their lives. The casualties of this tragic happening were Virgil Tanner and

Ira Yewell of Carterville, William (Bill) Gartner of Herrin, formerly of Carterville, George Alpha Horsley of Crainville, John Barkus, Melvin Ramsey, Howard Kimmel, and Roy Woodis of Herrin, Ralph Brandon and Ira Williams of Clifford. The mine was never reopened.

Two noted mine rescue workers, Ray McCluskey and Harry Carney, residents of Carterville, headed a brave rescue team to recover the unfortunate victims. Both McCluskey and Carney were on Madison Coal Company's "First Aid and Rescue Team" for a number of years, and in 1927 won first prize in combined rescue work at the National Convention in San Francisco, California. Throughout their mining experience they have assisted in many other mine disasters. Mr. McCluskey was an Illinois State Mine Inspector for twenty-five years, also.

For many years the tall smokestack of the old Clifford mine owned by the Big Muddy Coal and Iron Company could be seen standing as a silent sentinel of the prosperous as well as the sorrowful days in the once pleasant little mining village of Clifford, which boasted a large company store where a number of Carterville people worked. Allen Kilbreth, manager, Helen Peach, cashier and script clerk; and Marion Willis, bookkeeper, were in the main office. These commuted daily by jitney or taxi service. Oscar Bloodworth and Tom Holden were well known for this transportation service. In the period between 1918 and 1923 when there was no pavement extending north to Dewmaine, Colp, and Clifford, a treadway of boards extended quite some distance over a surface of cinders, with planks set edgewise on each side of North Division Street for the "jitneys" to drive upon as a precaution to keep the wheels on the treads and from sinking into the black gumbo. Margaret Bloodworth Chamness, daughter of Oscar Bloodworth, has informed me that her father had been a miner, but quit that vocation when there was such a demand from miners and others working at these three mining villages in near proximity to Carterville, because he could make more money running a jitney—5¢ each way. He drove a taxi many years.

Various deep-shaft mines closed down or were worked out. It has been said that where great noisy tipples had stood, after a lapse of some months weeds could be noted covering railroad sidings, and there were crumbling mine buildings, also abandoned houses. Scrub oaks were growing in silent mine yards, burntout slack piles were in much evidence, and here and there a smokestack standing alone in the middle of a field as at old Clifford.

Many of the residences at Clifford were torn down and hauled away in sections on big trucks—I have seen these loaded trucks myself passing on North Division during the Depression—and transported to Carbondale to be rebuilt by an enterprising realtor as an investment. He had literally "bought them for a song and sung it himself." I afterwards heard he had accumulated great wealth in this manner.

The largest mine to close down was near Cambria, the Madison No. 12. That, in so doing, threw many hundreds of miners out of work. I've been told it had the most modern mining equipment and machinery at that time. It is reported that in this mine a large room in the depth of its deep pit was known as the "banquet room," where the mine officials' table was set with white cloth and napkins and special dinnerware. There was a large lake or pond on the grounds above, stocked with fish provided for the recreational pleasure of the officials; and yearly summer picnics were held for them there. The lake still exists.

Early Industries of Carterville

Of no less importance than the miners in the settling of the town were the farmers who migrated here mainly from Kentucky and Tennessee and planted the crop with which they were most familiar—tobacco. This gave rise to the tobacco barns and the pressing of it into big hogsheads of the packed weed to be hauled to Marion, one of the greatest tobacco-

140

shipping points north of Kentucky, where teamsters hauled it thence to Carbondale, from where it was shipped to the tobacco marts of the world, much of it going to London, England. This was before the advent of railroads in the county. My grandfather, W. E. Sizemore, had settled on a large farm in 1864 just a short distance north, and only seven years before Carterville was born. He was a tobacco farmer. His wife Lucinda Cavanas Sizemore was noted for her weaving, especially wool coverlets, many of which she sold to residents in Carbondale and the area. She also wove on the large loom he had made for her in Tennessee, materials for the clothes of the family as well as blankets.

There was a woolen mill at Marion where she took wool, traveling over the old road through the Burr Woods and by Hurricane Church. The road was called the Pennyroyal Road, as many early settlers gathered that herb from the woods, and took it also to be sold in Marion for medicinal purposes.

I remember so well my mother telling how as a growing child it was her filial responsibility to wear a blue linsey-woolsey dress my grandmother had woven for the tobacco field and "worm" the tobacco leaves each day of the growing season, and what a hated task it was! If you have ever seen an ugly big green and yellow tobacco worm, you'll get the picture of her chore!

My mother was taught to weave, especially rag carpeting, and she was proud of the twenty-eight yards she wove the year I was born for the living-room floor of our home. It was common in those days for housewives to tack carpet rags and wind them in balls in readiness to use when the loom was threaded for use. She also told me the true story of how her mother wound into carpet-rag balls $400.00 from the sale of land in Tennessee, then stuffed the balls into a big hogshead for safekeeping as the family left their Southern home (due to dissension of the Civil War) to migrate to Illinois. My mother learned the art of piecing quilts and quilting when very young. She quilted numerous quilts for prominent ladies in our town even as late as the 1920's. I

141

was fascinated by the various patterns of quilt blocks that had such interesting names: Bear's Paw, Fox and Geese, Washington's Plume, Pickle Dish, Wedding Ring, Bow Tie, Lone Star, Sunburst, Friendship Jacob's Ladder and many others.

Quilting is still carried on by the Ladies' Aid of the First Christian Church here. Their work has gone to Chicago and other faraway places. Other women in the town and vicinity were equally skilled in these "home factory" crafts. Among them were Mrs. Mary Murphy, who resided many years on Nevada Street, next door west of Dr. Vick's residence. She was adept at weaving rag carpets and rag rugs, and supported herself in this manner many years.

Another home weaver was Mrs. Philander Bozarth—although most people called her "Granny Bozier." She resided in one of the few original log cabins of the town, at the corner of Olive and Anderson Street. She stands out in my childhood memory since, at the Christmas season Mr. James W. Turner, superintendent of our school, advised all the schoolchildren from first grade through the newly organized high school to bring gifts of fruits, vegetables, jellies and the like to the Widow Bozarth, which were carried over to her. When she died a few years later, all the teachers and students filed by her body, which lay in state in her humble cabin home. She loved flowers, and beautiful rose-bushes graced the doorway. Mrs. Elizabeth Bishop remembers her well, also, and has recently told me how the Hutton family loved her. She was a welcome guest to share Mrs. Hutton's good vegetable soup or other foods she had prepared. The cabin stood just across from the present residence of Mr. and Mrs. C. W. (Runt) Bishop. I feel fortunate to have received an original post-card picture of it mailed to Mrs. Merta Sonner in 1909 from Pearl Robinson, postal clerk in Carterville at that time. Mrs. Sonner has written saying that her father sold the first lot to Mr. Bozarth from the original forty-acre plot of the village. An old deed-record printed many years ago in the *Carterville*

Herald bears this out, perhaps. A copy of this yellowed item is as follows:

AN OLD DEED

Mrs. Maude Hampton in rummaging about in the files of her office, came across an old deed that may stir some memories. It is made by George and Ollie McNeill to Philander D. Bozarth on November 6, 1873. Carterville at that time was making a brave start and the Carbondale Coal and Coke Company was in operation."

This location is evidently where the first depot of Carterville was located at George McNeill's request mentioned earlier in this story.

A most unusual and unique industry in Carterville was developed on the Gartner homestead here a number of years ago by the father of William, Edward, Victoria, Emma, Marie, Helen and Hugo Gartner. This historic two story-home, which sat high on the hill where Dr. Fine's residence now stands, was torn down after Mrs. Gartner moved away. The Gartner sisters were all teachers and were noted for their beauty. Each had a regal bearing similar to their beautiful mother who, in her youth, it is said, was a lady in waiting to a noblewoman in her native Austria. With this background in mind, I will quote from a letter under date April 1, 1971 sent to me by Mrs. Victoria (Gartner) Richardson, now residing in Cannonsburg, Pennsylvania, in answer to my inquiry about her father's ginseng industry:

"No Foolin'! I'm finally writing to you about my dad and his ginseng. He read about the plant in his German newspaper from Lincoln, Nebraska, a weekly newspaper. He ordered his seeds, I don't know from where. They had to be covered with sand and allowed to germinate eighteen months outdoors. He buried seeds and sand outdoors in the garden. The seeds looked like cherry seeds—very hard.

"He had to prepare the proper shade, so he arranged tall posts in rows and put heavy wire for roofing, over which he

143

laid branches for shade. He had bought a small twenty-acre farm southeast of town which had black loam soil. He took that black loam and mixed it with our clay soil and planted the ginseng in rows when it was a foot tall. The plant is called Panax Quinque Folium (like a spread-out hand is the leaf shape.) The leaves are a deep green and a cluster of small flowers is at the top of the plant. Yellow Paccoon is grown among the ginseng to take the diseases which would attack and ruin the 'seng,' Gold Seal is another name for yellow Paccoon—we raised that plant also among the 'seng.'

" 'Pop' had a book which he ordered from Washington County, Pennsylvania all about the wild ginseng which grows in the woods hereabouts. Our roots were harvested after seven years but we never had much for shipment and the market was not too good at the time our 'seng' was ready, due to internal struggle in China and that area. We shipped through St. Louis exporters and through New York exporters.

"When 'Pop' was sent home from the hospital in St. Louis he drank tea from ginseng (boiled, ground-up roots with a little wintergreen or mint for flavor, as it is rather bitter to taste.) His health improved and he returned two or three times—had the doctors puzzled. They couldn't understand why he didn't pass away when he was sent home. He had carcinoma of the lungs, and this caused him to expectorate blood in rather large amounts. Ginseng is good for the blood system, so he drank the tea—prolonged his life a little, at least we think so."

Mr. Gartner had worked in the mines for many years, but his venture in growing this rare plant in the long-shaded plot back of his home was a curiosity to the citizens for years. It is significant at this point to mention that his son William, who was previously mentioned, lost his life in the Blue Blaze mine.

In writing of the history of the Gartner house, Victoria in her letter further stated that Laban Carter (co-founder of Carterville) built the house—and when they moved into it there was a picture of him hanging in the hall, but it went

144

with the house when the property was sold to Dr. Fine. To this she added, "Other prior occupants were Mr. and Mrs. Rudy Phillips, parents of Lorena and Evan Phillips, and then it was owned by the McCutcheon family, who in turn sold it to Gartners."

Mention must be made of the J. B. Venable Dairy at the Venable farm that was in operation for many years at the south edge of the city limits. Glass milk bottles were the mode of that day.

Carterville Belles in Gay Nineties
Front row, l. to r.: Jessie Roach; Belle Lockie (later Mrs. George Hall; still later Mrs. T. P. Russell); Lizzie Watson (later Mrs. Fred Richart); unidentified; Maude Stotlar (later wife of Dr. Alloway); rear: Jessie Wagner, Annie Kennedy.

CHAPTER IX

HEALTH AND ENTERTAINMENT

1. *Pertaining to Communicable Diseases and Doctors*

Many children of my generation going to school wore a small bag of assefetida on a string or ribbon around their necks, and I was no exception. This bitter drug with a persistent odor was believed by our elders to counteract or ward off germs of whooping cough, measles, chicken pox, diptheria, scarlet fever, and the like. The little bag was worn all through the fall, winter, and spring months, and by that time it had become quite slick. No doubt its obnoxious odor kept others at an appreciable distance, but nevertheless the taboo was practiced here in the early 1900's.

Carterville, however, was proud of its Board of Health, on which a prominent doctor served faithfully; and if there was a symptom of an epidemic, this board acted promptly, placing red signs on the residences to be quarantined and checking on the proper fumigation in the homes when restrictions were over.

The most dreaded disease, no doubt, was smallpox. Vaccinations were not common then in this town. An epidemic of that terrible malady broke out in 1903. It was most severe, especially in the vicinity of Herrin, just six miles distant, causing much suffering and many deaths. Churches there were closed for three months.

Uncle Abe Whitecotton and his wife Nancy, who were well known in Carterville and vicinity, were victims. Nancy died and he lost an eye. The Herrin Baptist Church, of which they were members, was draped for two months in memory of Nancy and another victim, Mrs. Joplin. I am indebted to

146

Miss Mable McNeill for this account recorded in the history of that church.

I am relating at this point a bit of story which links in with my memory about the smallpox epidemic of that year. There was a very large white oak tree that stood on the W. E. Sizemore farm where it joined the Henry Phillips acreage, and it was a landmark for many years at the north corporate limits of the City of Carterville. A stile of five or six steps had been built on either side of the fence for the convenience of people walking into town or returning. There was a two-plank board walk extending to the corporate limits. My brother and I often went to our grandfather's and used the stile. Sometime that summer as we were approaching it, we noticed a tent stretched in the shade of that white oak and a man on guard there. He was Cave Watson, brother of our neighbor, "Little Tobe" Watson. He had been hired by the city authorities of Carterville to keep watch lest anyone slip by coming from the north road via Colp and Dewmaine, a possible escapee from the "pest house" where small-pox victims were. We learned, too, from our parents that persons who had died of the malady and were to be buried in our Oakwood cemetery could not be brought into the city except at night-time. This was Mr. Watson's duty—to keep accurate and constant check.

Between 1910 and 1914 there were several severe cases of typhoid fever here. Again, no known vaccine at the time. I fell victim in the fall of 1914, and it was several months before I could walk again. My hair all fell out, too. My mother had fastened a sheet over the mirror of my chifforobe so I could not see myself when I became able to sit up. She removed it when I had gained strength to walk in the room. On looking at myself in it for the first time, I exclaimed, "Mama, do you know what I look like?" I went on laughingly, "My neck looks like a goose-neck hoe holding my head up." To this she laughed also, but she knew I was literally skin and bones. Dr. Aird was the doctor who treated me during this critical illness.

147

Other dreaded diseases of this period were scarlet fever and diphtheria, which claimed the lives of several children here. By the 1930's when I was teaching, vaccines were administered to the children and teachers, too. Also typhoid immunization was given.

I have already mentioned some of the earlier medical doctors and dentists of Carterville who served the people in this community so creditably. There are many of a later period that should be included. Here are some of them: Dr. Huff, Dr. Foster, Dr. McCandless, Dr. Whitacre, and Dr. White. A later physician, who came after World War II, was Dr. Hugh McGowan. He later moved to Carbondale. Notable dentists not previously mentioned were Dr. Langstead, Dr. Entsminger, Dr. Lloyd Bevard, Dr. Frank Washburn, and Dr. M. A. Shively.

2. *Entertainment, "Low-Brow" to "High-Brow"*

Before the days of the nickelodeon there were periodic medicine shows—usually set up for a week of nightly performances—between the Carterville State and Savings Bank and the Elles Store. There was nearly always a banjo player, sometimes in blackface, and also a "barker" who extolled the wonders of Wizard Oil, and bitters guaranteed to cure any kind of ailment. Most were sold from 25¢ to $1.00. This medicine show filled a gap that would otherwise have been a dull existence.

Then there were the usual yearly carnival shows that located in the City Park. The iridescent, brightly colored bowls, glasses, and such were given as prizes at some of the stands; also "Kewpie Dolls." We were unaware in those days that by the 1970's Carnival glass would be collectors' items.

Circuses were common, too. The first one I remember was the Van Amberg Circus. We children in the Park Addition called it the "Van Humbug" Circus, but I'm sure we didn't give it its proper due, as it had a wonderful long parade which went over the principal streets. It was so amusing to watch with the beautiful horses and their riders, elephants and clowns following the gaudy, glittering bandwagon, while in their train came a real steam calliope playing hauntingly.

The most noted big tent show to come to Carterville was Buffalo Bill's Wild West Show, which performed at the corner of Prosperity Street and VanWyck Avenue. The date was a short time prior to the turn of the century. The late Leo Watson went to see it when a young boy. Buffalo Bill (William Cody) had gained fame with his famous "Congress of the rough Riders of the World" in many of the capitals of Europe, and had appeared at two command performances before Queen Victoria, the latter one in 1892, besides in the leading large cities of our country. Therefore it must be concluded that, with his army of Indian braves, which included Kicking Bear, Short Bull and twenty-five rebellious Sioux leaders with wild steers, wild buffaloes, cowboys and noted plainsmen, he must have considered Carterville a likely place to bring his "Frontier Day" performance. In 1893, he had taken his show to the Chicago World's Fair. One should read *Stirring Lives of Buffalo Bill and Pawnee Bill* by Frank Cooper for the complete story of the Congress of the Rough Riders of the World.

The last circus, perhaps, to perform in Carterville was the Miller Brothers' Circus during the Depression. It, too, was in the park, but there was no parade. The schoolchildren were delighted to see it.

While on the subject of circuses, there is a true incident sent to me a few months ago by Victor Morris of Denver, Colorado who, with his parents, brothers, and sisters, resided here prior to 1909. Victor's father was a mine official of Old Prosperity. The street-car line was novel to everyone then. A circus was billed to show in Marion; and Reverend Fidler was the pastor of the Methodist Church here, of which the Morris family were members. The minister invited the Morris children to go with him on the street car to see the afternoon circus performance. So Mrs. Morris thought it would be quite a treat for them, and her children were allowed to go. By the following Sunday, however, word had spread among the parishioners that the good reverend was a "show-goer," and there arose almost a tumult of criticism which took a while for him to calm from his pulpit.

In the early 1920's, Ringling Brothers' Circus passed through Carterville by train on its way to Marion, and of course many people went to see this "greatest show on earth" since it was so near. That night a terrible electrical and wind storm came, and a great number of people had much difficulty getting back to Carterville over the muddy roads. Other circuses such as Hagenback, Sells Floto, and Foupaugh flaunted their large, gaudy signs on country barns. billboards, and high fences, advertising their circus dates in the neighboring larger towns.

After the period of stage shows in Samuel's Opera House and the traveling vaudeville circuits, the Chautauquas were the popular mode of entertainment for several summers in Carterville. Very recently I have read an article released by the National Geographic Society stating that, "Traveling Chautauquas took to the road in 1904, pitching tents and presenting lecture programs leavened with operatic divas, magic acts, and ventriloquists. By 1909 there were five hundred fifty-four Chautauquas making the rounds, and 'Chautauqua time' had become the high point of the summer in towns and villages across the country. Audiences in straw hats, and waving hand-fans against the summer heat, heard Swiss Bellringers, Hawaiian guitarists and Madame Schumann-Heink singing Schubert. Radio, motion pictures, and the Great Depression of 1929 ended the circuit. As Theodore Roosevelt, one of the seven United States President to speak at Chautauqua, said of an earlier summer session. "It will be a gathering that is typically American. . . ." This article further states, "Traveling Chautauquas are making a comeback."

This all brings to my mind the summer of 1909, when Carterville's first Chautauqua was held here under a big tent among the beautiful, big oak trees in the City Park. My father was one of the sponsors, and it was a responsibility of each sponsor to provide lodging and two meals (supper and break-fast) for the performing artists. It fell his lot to give this service to the dwarf singing sisters, Lucy and Sarah Adams, listed on the scheduled program as the "Lilliputian Sisters" —their height being 38 inches and 36 inches respectively. I can never forget how interesting they were as they adjusted themselves to our simple mode of life with no city water or bathroom accommodations during the hours before and after their evening performance. They were natives of Massachusetts and claimed lineage from the John Quincy Adams Family. On the program that night they sang and acted out a charming number, which title has left me, but the chorus was hauntingly plaintive with the closing words—"Come this way, Papa!"— in blended, sweetly childish tones, befitting their miniature stature. The next morning they walked to the depot to catch the early train for Kinmundy, the next town on the circuit. John Crowther, our neighbor, snapped their pictures with his Brownie Kodak as they were passing the Rufus Talley home on VanWyck Avenue. They heard the click and exclaimed. "Oh, you got us, didn't you!"

About 1911 another Chautauqua tent was set up on the lot just east of the old post office—a parking lot it is now. Although Madame Schumann-Heink did not appear here, she did give a concert in Herrin at the Marlow Theatre in the early 1920's which was well-advertised here and some of my friends purchased advance tickets at Vick Drug Store, boarding the street car to go hear her that evening. The outstanding program of the 1911 Chautauqua to me was a distinguished handsome lecturer from India and the beautiful songs, especially "On the Road to Mandalay" and "The Rosary," so popular at that time.

'A skating rink came to town in 1916, and the big tent was on the lot by the post office. It was a great attraction for young and old alike.

Now a word about the first radio I ever saw and heard. It was perhaps about 1921 or 1922 that a man brought a radio, giving a public program in the First Christian Church here. There were earphones provided for the listeners. All who paid to listen-in at this novel invention felt it was not worth the price of admission, due to the great amount of static. Not long afterwards several people were buying their own, with individual earphones. The Elmer Beasley family had bought one just prior to the national Presidential election and invited friends to listen in at the returns.

About 1928 I enjoyed listening in on an Atwater-Kent, a three-dial model having a horn-shaped loudspeaker. It was a table model in my Uncle Wilson Sizemore's home where I had gone to live. Such programs featuring "Lum and Abner" in their Jot-em-Down Store, "Amos and Andy," Fibber and Molly McGee," also "Twenty Mule Team Borax" stories of Death Valley were popular evening entertainment for Aunt Mary and me on the long winter nights affording actual "homespun" humor that was table-talk at many a breakfast table the next morning.

Carterville had its share of stock companies giving their three-act plays, with comedians and singers and orchestra performing between acts. Notable were Curtis-Shankland, Choate's, and the Billie Terrell Stock Company, each of which set up their tents with some reserved seats and the "chicken roost" next to the old post office. A crumbling, yellowed page of the Carterville Herald published on October 6, 1922 shows an advertisement as follows:

ALL WEEK   OCTOBER 9-14
CURTIS-SHANKLAND STOCK COMPANY
BAND AND ORCHESTRA
—ACTS "THE DOLLAR POWER"
POPULAR PRICES   DOORS OPEN 7:15 P.M.
TENT LOCATED NEXT TO POST OFFICE

Some of these stock companies came to town for several years, they were so popular with the people. Choate's wintered in Cambria.

Carterville has always been proud of its musical interests, especially the orchestras and bands, even to the present time.

By delving back into W. F. Wilcox's *Souvenir History of Williamson County* (1905) I find that the First Baptist Church had an orchestra of eleven pieces and twenty-two additional singers, with Dr. J. H. Brooks, leader, and Will Peebles, assistant and first cornet; Arthur Baker, 1st cornet; Vern Allen, 2nd cornet; Miss Lucy Jones, 1st violin; David Crowder, 2nd violin; Sam Hodges, flute; Raymond Jones, flute; Lloyd Walker, trombone; Lacy Peyton, trombone; George Pressley, bass cello; Miss Bessie Jones, organist. This item concludes, "Under the able and scientific leadership of Dr. Brooks, finer church music has never been produced in the state than the people of Carterville are favored with every Sunday."

There was another noted orchestra in the town about this period. A beautiful photo taken inside the Gunster parlor shows the members with their instruments: Jim Taylor, trombone; Richard Hadfield, cornet; John King, clarinet; Miss Josie Gunster, pianist; Alex McCrae, violin; Robert Porrit, violin; and his father, Tom Porrit, bass violin. A few of these members were also in Sizemore's Concert Band.

The first article I began to write was about the famed Sizemore Band. Since then I have acquired some photographs of this band and its predecessor, the Gunster Cornet Band, which is worthy of mention here to identify their membership. Those in the Gunster Band were Leo Gunster, Bob Liddell, G. W. (Billy) Bevard, Joe Kelley, Will McEwan, Will Thompson, Joe Hadfield, Wilson Sizemore, Chester Taylor, Bill Liddell, Frank Sizemore, and Peter Gunster.

One picture of Sizemore's Band (taken by the side of a building) shows Ed Boyd, Hiram Rice, Jim Taylor, Bob Hadfield, Arlie Wolfenbarger, Joe Hadfield, John Rowatt, Tom Porrit, Minor Braswell, Jim Hutton, Will Peebles, Dick Hadfield, Alex Richardson, Alex McCrae, Bennie Sizemore, and Louis Crowder. The other photo of this band was taken in the City Park just after one of the annual Fourth of July celebrations and shows Tom Porrit, Will McEwan, Jim Taylor, John Rowatt, Jim Hutton, Dick Hadfield, Alex McCrae,

Chester Taylor, Frank Sizemore (conductor), Ed Sizemore, Billie Swaar, Hiram Rice, Charlie Dunn, and John King.

In the early 1940's a later Carterville orchestra gained prominence locally at church and social functions. It met for regular practices in the Methodist church here and was directed by H. Bernice Mason, a prominent letter-carrier for many years, also a champion checker-player, having won the Illinois Checker Championship Tournament once and the 101 Counties Tournament three times. He has been a private music teacher and still enjoys playing the violin. Other violin players in this orchestra were Mrs. Letha Ledbetter, Mrs. Myrtle Beasley and son Bill, the late Clara Lockie, and the piano accompanist, the late Mrs. Pearl Baker. Dick Richardson also directed.

I have kept over the years two programs in a series of "Three Musicals" sponsored by the Carterville Woman's Club, no admission but a free-will offering for the Red Cross. The first one, home talent, was held on March 16, 1942 at the Methodist Church; the other was on December 6, 1943 at the First Baptist Church. At these performances in the cultural interest of the town, the local orchestra happily shared its talents for the pleasure of the audiences. Mrs. Frank (Letha) Ledbetter, wife of the *Carterville Herald* editor, a musician of note herself, arranged these programs and brought other talented folk, particularly young people from surrounding towns, to appear on some of her programs.

There was a most distinctive and unique mode of entertainment during the Depression years that happened annually on Halloween. It was a parade of decorated children's wagons with beautiful pre-school children dressed so prettily riding in them and being pulled along Division Street in the business district by intermediate boys and girls. The parade was sponsored by the merchants, and prizes were awarded to the outstanding ones. A particular theme was carried out for these miniature floats. Two outstanding ones were "popular songs" and "historic poems of American history." I believe little golden haired, blue-eyed Mary Joan McCluskey, daughter of

154

John and Maud McCluskey, won first in the popular song category being sponsored by Hampton Drug Store. An outstanding float in the historic poem was one pertaining to the signing of the Declaration of Independence when in 1776 the Liberty Bell was rung and the sexton in the steeple of Independence Hall awaited the signal of his little grandson down below to shout 'Ring! Grandpa, ring!" Little Malcolm (Sonny) McNeill was a fourth-grader at that time and portrayed so well the small lad in his three-cornered hat over a white wig, and wearing a matching blue suit in colonial style. William Thetford, the grade-school custodian, had silvered an old dinner bell, and we teachers had completed the final decorations. All the floats were made and assembled in the Holmes Garage. Hundreds of people from all over the area came to view these novel parades. Big, little, old, and young participated, too, in masking for these occasions, and the city square was alive with them. Much wholesome merriment reigned. After the judging of floats and costumed people, a street square-dance followed. This now brings me up to the relating of some humorous folklore.

CHAPTER X

A TOWN OF PRANKS OR PRACTICAL JOKES

G. D. Wallace has stated that he, no doubt, contributed a lot to Carterville's being known over many states at one time as the "Town of Pranks," when as a youth he sold papers and yelled many a headline on which no story existed. He would open the door of a barber shop and yell out the headline. Caught as a buyer in one of these headline dragnets was a stranger called "Ring Lardner." So amused he was when he discovered it was a town of pranksters that he stayed for several days at the Carterville Hotel, and all the barbers from Wayne McCamish to Bill Gallimore and Frank Sizemore kept him amused with stories, never dreaming he was a famous writer of short stories.

Almost every barber shop was the main attraction of the town. Through years of practice the highly skilled barbers became the greatest of pranksters and story-tellers. Topping the list was Bill Gallimore. At one time he agreed to let cherry trees be picked by a group of boys on the 50-50 split. The boys got huge tubs and long ladders and went to Bill's house to discover only one scrawny tree which bore only a few ripe cherries. Frank Sizemore was also tops in being a prankster, as well as Henry McCabe and the McCamish clan.

Doc (Elbert) Burress, who tended the front chair in Sizemore's shop, acquired the name of "Doc" because he was called out many times to shave the sick in their home or to shave a deceased person. He carried a small dark bag, similar to a doctor's satchel of that time, and thus he was finally pegged as a doctor.

Valentine's Day was a big affair, especially in the low-key

156

vein, and the most popular valentine was the comic one that sold for a penny. Most everyone got their share of these horrible cards. Again I quote from Gilbert D. Wallace: "The distributor of these cards was from St. Louis and their representative for Illinois told me they sold more cards of this type in the Carterville area than any town its size in Illinois. These cards were designed to furnish fun, but instead created many a rift as people tried to identify the handwriting to decide who hated them badly enough to send the greeting." I can substantiate that this was really a Valentine custom during my teaching career, and if the recipient had a sense of humor it helped!

Now there is another story of a practical joke Gilbert Wallace himself played on Frank Cox (the barber), who was serious, seldom given to a prank or joke. I quote again: "For years a certain salesman from Williams Soap Company had tried to persuade him to try his product. Mr. Cox wouldn't, however, consider changing until one day I told Bill Gallimore I liked Williams Soap the best and thought it lathered faster. Cox then purchased a box of ten bars to try.

"I noted his bar in the mug was almost ready to be replaced. That night, taking a turnip, I carved it into a replica of a bar of Williams Soap after I noted Mr. Cox at the end of his day's business had inserted in the mug a brand-new bar to try it out. I had everything arranged, including Mr. Cox's first customer the next morning. Next morning he was standing by. While Cox was sweeping out, I substituted the bar I had carved. In popped the customer in a rush, wanting a quick shave. 'I have a very prompt appointment in fifteen minutes,' he said 'and if you can get me finished in that time, there is a dollar tip!' Quickly Mr. Cox gave his straight razor a fifteen-second strop on the leather belt. He let the hot water pour over the mug, and then, plunging in the brush, set up the swirl pattern to bring up the dense foam. The only foam that arrived was from what was left in the brush from the day's-before business. Cox turned the heat fully on and tried again with less success. His customer now fidgeted in the seat, saying, 'I've just got to get going.' Cox looked at the clock. Time was running out. All at once, his customer jumped up, jerked off the apron and dashed out the door. Mr. Cox looked amazed. Then he looked at me and muttered, 'You and your William's Soap!' Disgusted, he fished out the turnip and flung it out the door. Then he got the box of soap which still contained nine bars and flung it the distance across the street. Then he went across the street to Hampton Drug Store and bought another bar of his old faithful soap."

No wonder old Ring Lardner was fascinated by the barber shop and the pranks that seemed to center there.

A story Merta Sonner has sent me concerns a prank to test who was the laziest man in town—a prominent doctor or an equally noted editor. It was agreed that each would be offered a dollar bill for the test. So the currency was taken to the editor's office, but the editor did not pick it up but said, "Just lay it on the counter." Next, the village doctor was approached with a dollar bill and asked if he would like to have it, to which he replied, "Yes, please put it in my shirt pocket." From this it is easy to conclude the lazier of the two.

I have mentioned the old two-story frame red schoolhouse facing West Grand Avenue. There was a boarding house just west of it on Oak Street across from the school. It was known as the Matthew's house—the owner Tom Matthews, who always raised a fine garden. Mr. Matthews took pride in taking a market basket of fresh vegetables in the morning to peddle to the nearby groceries on South Division Street, but he was a man seemingly afraid of everything and looked on the gloomy side of life. So, when one April Fool's Day rolled around (about 1895), the storekeepers made it up that morning that each of them would stand outside their shops as he came along and tell him how bad he looked. Sure enough, he was told this so many times that he turned back and hurried to his home and went right to bed, telling his wife he was very sick! This bit of folklore is an actual fact, according to Roxanna Snyder.

Odd Fellows and Rebekahs Marching to Convention
It is thought the picture may have been taken after a disastrous fire on
North Division Street, prior to 1900.

Carterville Tigers

Standing, l. to r.: Ray Atkins, referee from Anna, Ill.; Eph Evett, halfback; Leo Watson, tackle; Speedy Hastie, fullback; Harrison Colp, halfback; Earl Parks, umpire from Marion, Ill.; Fern "Monk" Evett, lineman. Kneeling, l. to r.: unidentified; Audie Burnett, center and guard; Lloyd "Onion Head" Russell, tackle; Guy Eveland, guard; Cline Ghent, guard and center; Elbert "Fat" True, tackle and fullback (Marion); Harry Carr, halfback and end; Harry "Chicken" Crain, end. Lying down, l. to r.: Lynn Kimbro, quarterback; John McNeill, halfback and end; Joe Kelley, guard and center; Stanley Tuberville, halfback; C. W. "Runt" Bishop, quarterback and end.

The "New" Depot About 1910
It is thought that E. H. Harriman, the railroad magnate, came to Carterville for the dedication.

Quotable Nicknames

The late Paul Rowatt, a native of Carterville, sent me a letter from Chicago under date of June 6, 1967, from which I quote the following:

John Town, Inc.
(Formerly Dana, Perfumes, Inc.)

I am enclosing a list of the "400" from Carterville. I am sure you will remember some of them better than I. Some are better known by these names than others—but they all lived in and around Carterville.

When I came to Chicago in 1924 I did not know one person here, but since that time a lot of people have moved away—Chicago, Florida and California—and when I meet some of them naturally we talk about what now seems to be old times. The old folks die and the young move away. I used to ask the young ones coming to Chicago, 'Who are your folks?'—and now I ask, 'Who are your grandparents?' I suppose the Burr C closing made a big difference in Carterville, even to the extent that no one grows cabbage like the days when I used to deliver groceries for Elles Store. Don't forget a copy (your book) for me.

Paul

From Paul's list of literally "The Four Hundred of Carterville" are the following:

"Red Peck" Adams
"Lollie (Wooden Ears)" Aird
"Egg Counter" Barwick
"Business" Baxter
"Soup" Bellett
"Whee Whaa" Burkholtz
"Fuzzle Gut" Graddock
"Dynamite" Black
"Jug Head" Boren
"Hobble" Boswell
"Lobster (Lob)" Calhoun
"Daniel Boone" Carter
"Egg Head" Cochran
"Zappy" Moulton
"Crap Face" Craig
"Yaller Bill" Crain
"Possum" Dollar
"Ham Fat" Eaton

"Budgie" Ferrill
"Little Boo" Fozzard
"Chaw Waa" Gentry
"Feather Head" Gentry
"Grunt Nose" Ghent
"Big Skin" Halstead
"Fuzzy" Harris
"Poker Jim" Harris
"Smiley" Hastie
"Scrubby" Hatfield
"Tom Plug" Hatfield
"Hercules," "Skinny," "Sis," and
    "Slop" Heckel
"Paddle Foot" Holmes
"Koosome" Impson
"Bouncer" Jeffery
"Dipper Handle" Jackson
"Squib" Jernigan

159

"Double Head" Johnson	"Froggie" Rutherford
"Drumhead" Kelley	"Chalk" Samuel
"Vampire" Kemp	"Jerker" Sizemore
"Hawkshaw" Lauder	"Old Spider" Spicer
"Tom Bean" Lauder	"Tang" Talley
"Hookum" McCamish	"Cuckleburr" Tanner
"Whiffeloo" Noakes	"Hoodie" Taylor
"Diz" Phillips	"Beefy" Tregoning
"Pie Face" Phillips	"Gobbo" Tregoning
"Shorty" Presley	"Little Sand Pig" Underwood
"Bean Eye" Randolph	"Punch" Tregoning
"Squat" Richardson	"Squinney" Wagley
"Big Enough" Roberts	"Whistle Dick" Waldron
"Banty" Rowatt	"Jelly Bean" Walker
"Stud Duck" Rowatt	"Spoon Heel" Wall
"Onion Head" Russell	"Banjo Eyes" McCain

CHAPTER XI

BITS, PIECES AND SOME WIT OF YESTERYEAR

The following excerpts from the *Carterville Herald,* July 9, 1954, from the pen of Frank Ledbetter, editor, relate to early teachers and salaries listed in records of the township Treasurer. This newspaperman scanned:

B. T. and W. H. Bundy show up in 1871 and Warren Hill, Salley Oliver and Arabel Hayton. In 1870 the names of G. W. Young, C. H. Dennison and W. Sanford Gee appear. Dennison had to do with the first bank in Carterville.

In the book is a note where Laban Carter furnished coal for Fifteen Dollars in 1870, when coal began to start Carterville on its way and the mining section of Williamson County.

Reuben Fozard taught for several teachers in 1873; J. M. Washburn, for C. L. Washburn; A. H. North taught for P. R. Baker that year. W. H. Perry taught the year of 1873.

William Hayton, teaching in 1875. There is a note that William Tranbarger took an order for Alice Tranbarger—she with W. H. Bundy teaching in 1871 or 1872. The township treasurer drew Forty Dollars for keeping the records. Martha Stocks and James Chenowith, teachers in 1875.

In 1878 there are the names of Ben L. Washburn for Forty Dollars, also Martha Stocks, Alice Painter, Minnie White and Mary Reeves. Ben L. Washburn must have taught quite a while, his name shows up often. He was later postmaster of Carterville. Average salary Thirty Dollars per month, and he was one of the better teachers.

In 1891 school orders listed were for Marion Watson, Kate Winning, Lydia Owen and George White. In 1894, names of Calla L. Vick, Daisy Baker, and Frank L. Shreve appear. Grant Peterson seems to have been a regular then. Martha A. Birkholz's name also appears.

There seems to be a jump from 1902 to 1907, where names like these show up: Cecil Baker, Minnie Owens, Mae Davis, Ora Crain, Mable Womack, Lena Whitacre, J. L. Parks and E. G. Lentz. Lentz was principal. His check was for $86.07. (It is to be noted, he later

161

was on the faculty for many years at Southern Illinois Normal University in Carbondale. He is attributed to have said "I was the one who brought civilization to Carterville.") In that year also appears Agnes L. Stewart.

H. L. Atwood appears in 1910, also P. H. Leaman, Julian Atwood, Bessie Washburn, Zella West, Clara Stocks, Kate Vick, Ella Bandy, Florence Adams, Minnie Greer, J. W. Kimbro, Della Adams, and others.

R. G. Crisenberry, a schoolman who left his mark in this town, appears about 1911. He is state senator and lives at Murphysboro and still has a fondness for Carterville, Kate Dowell appears, who was Kate Winning earlier. One of the best-loved teachers of her time, and yet quite firm, Carrie Russell is listed. Roger Tippy shows up about 1912, probably starting his first school. Mable Canaday also appears.

Firms like Burklow and Cooksey appear in 1913, and North and McNeill lumberers. That's a new word—but then, that is what the book says, lumberers.

Miss Kate Ferrell shows up on the records about this time; her sister, Miss Minnie Ferrell, started earlier. An L. L. Jones and a George Damron appear, and Etta Neely and Amos Taylor. There is a C. K. Schuey and C. E. ·Baker, too, and he's maybe the Schuey who established the Schuey orchard south of Marion. Edith Sutton appears, too, about this time, and there is Roxy Snyder and Laura Crain. Lena Beasley appears about 1914 or 1915, and there is a F. J. Coleman listed.

O. A. Towns succeeded Crisenberry, if a page or two were not missed in the record.

In 1917 the faculty must have been something like this: Bess Washburn, Clara Watt, Margaret Gooden, Laura Crain, Inez Anderson and Ruth Hampton (Washburn), Laura Russell, Lena Beasley, Maude Spires, Docie Vaughn, Roxy Snyder, Edna Bevard, Minnie Greer, Agnes Stewart, Mae Hughes, Rebecca Davis, Gloria G. Ralph, Vida A. Kerr, J. L. Corzine, O. A. Towns (Supt.), and possibly John Hancock was custodian.

In 1920 names like Ruth Rowatt, Lottie Elders, Zoe McNeill, Beatrice Baker, and Ruth Lauder appear.

The last entry in 1920 in one of the books, now thirty-four years old, lists Libby Moulton, John L. Spires, Anna Payne, Willie Shockley, Emma Vaughn, Mary Batson, R. H. Finley, Fay Crain, Edna McGinnis, Claude Cox, G. G. Choate, Lillie Stroud, Beatrice Baker, Maude Spires, Agnes Etewart, Mrs. Mae Proudley, Kate Dowell, Osa Tygett, Minnie Greer, Kate Ferrell, Anna Burton, Lottie Elders, Vada Greer, Ruth Rowatt, Violet Wagner, Cavanas Scoby, and Ruth Lauder. A Troy Kesley and Hope Crain are listed, too, and Kate Bradbury. Some of these taught rural schools.

And the salaries were around seventy and seventy-five dollars for the most part.

And as people read these names there will be many who recall them. Schoolteachers over a period of twenty-five or thirty years touch nearly every family in a community.

And this is part of the record from 1870 to 1920. Many will read and memories will return thick and fast.

The reference to Warren Hill listed here in 1871 recalls to my memory that he taught the school that my mother attended in her childhood here. She told me it was a log schoolhouse and the pupils sat on puncheon seats. A puncheon was a log split in half, holes bored in it, and legs inserted. The split half was turned up and smoothed none too well, so there were many splinters. Incidentally, Warren Hill was the father of Florence Hill (Swan) who taught many years here, and Mrs. Cloyd (Anna) Coleman, also a well-known teacher.

A Sidewalk of Names

The broad and curving concrete sidewalk leading from South Division Street up to the many-stepped entrance to the Carterville Community High School is most unique, and probably none other similar to it exists.

It is fitting, at this point, to mention a quote from Carterville High School Black Diamond—1925, which gives a resume of the difficulties encountered in completing this new building.

"The present members of the school board, L. G. Crain, President; Fred Richart, Secretary; Arthur A. Alexander; James R. Watson and John L. Spires have served continuously for the last five years. We have not the room here to give the complete history of this period or the work the board had done. Nearly everyone is familiar with the trouble undergone in maintaining the High School District and in completing the new building. Since the Community District was first organized in 1919 there has been a series of elections, trials and court proceedings. In every election the high school won out. In the early court proceedings the objectors were defeated. Then the territory south of Crab Orchard Creek and that part in West Marion Township petitioned to withdraw from the district. The right to withdraw was granted and the district seemed almost destroyed. Persisting, however, the board appealed to the State Supreme Court and were successful in putting the district on a sound basis again. The story of the new building would occupy pages, but we will only say here that the building was constructed over all opposition and has been in use over a year.

"The Carterville Community High School District is in fact now on a better financial basis than the surrounding districts. The school board cannot be given too much praise for their efforts in behalf of higher education in Carterville."

In regard to the sidewalk I mentioned, many citizens and business people in town by popular subscription and donations had this unique walk built showing names of firms, prominent children of prominent people, and the various graduating class rolls from 1903 into the 1920's stamped in the concrete so all posterity could see. What a pity some of the blocks have been broken up or destroyed, obliterating many of the historic names. Don't you think a movement should be started to restore them? If you haven't noticed this walk along the maple avenue, you should, for it will give you a nostalgic feeling for "Our Dear Old High."

Halley's Comet

I wonder who remembers the excitement and uneasy anticipation about the appearance of Halley's Comet in May, 1910? Everyone in town from schoolchildren to adults seemingly was talking about it, and probably the most fearful of them was a man named Charles B. Scott, a painter and paperhanger by trade, who lived in our neighborhood. He was afraid that when the earth passed through the comet's long tail on the predicted date, May 19, 1910, the world might come to an end. Its anticipated passage once every seventy-five years had been widely publicized by newspapers, and many people became uneasy over the prospect of the poi-

164

sonous gases, known by astronomers to be in the comet's tail, contaminating our atmosphere with dire consequences of light. Night after night Mr. Scott sat on his porch on Prosperity Street scanning the sky. Unfortunately, brilliant moonlight on the night of the passage prevented the seeing of any faint illumination in the firmament which might have come as consequence. According to information gleaned from the *Encyclopedia Americana,* I have learned that between April 19, 1910 and May 19, 1910 the comet was observed with telescopes of every kind, and literally thousands of visual observations and photographs were made. As it comes back four times every three centuries, naturally it has often appeared near some historical event connected there to by our superstitious ancestors. Examples—66 A.D., presaging the destruction of Jerusalem; 451 A.D., defeat of Attila and the Huns; 1006, the Norman Conquest; and 1456, peril of the Turks after the conquest of Constantinople. At this latter date the comet was so feared that Pope Calixtus III ordered special prayers to be offered for deliverance "from the devil, the Turk, and the Comet!" It is the only comet now known which will return during the rest of the century. It should return about 1985.

So perhaps painter Scott was more aware of these superstitions than any of his neighbors and felt justified in his fear!

Tornadoes

The Great Tornado, March 18, 1925, known as the most serious in the history of the United States, just missed Carterville by a few miles. That afternoon as I was walking home from the Park School I had great difficulty in keeping my feet on the sidewalk. That very evening our family was invited to a birthday supper for Mr. Rufus Talley at his house across from our home. As we were assembled around the dining table, Mr. Talley's son Arthur and Lloyd Noakes, a nephew, came and reported that news had come downtown that DeSoto was blown away and a great part of Murphysboro. These young men immediately left by car to find out more about it. Excitement reigned. Next morning, Mrs. Frank (Marie) Williams, one of our local teachers, who lived just two blocks from us, telephoned to me to tell that eleven relatives of hers and Frank's in DeSoto had been brought to the Williams home, since their homes were completely destroyed; and, too, there were several of her kin who had been killed in the terrible storm. There was an urgent need for clothing, especially, as well as other necessities. Marie's seventy-six-year-old Grandmother Heiple lay in the Holden Hospital, injured. I went over a few days later with Marie to see her, and there weren't enough rooms to accommodate the sorrowful victims. The corridors were filled. Appeals went out all over for clothing of all sizes to be sent to West Frankfort, the distributing center. People generously responded. My mother had passed away on March 2, just sixteen days before, and my father and I gladly gave most of her clothing for Grandma Heiple when she was released from the hospital to stay in the Williams home until the Red Cross could rehabilitate.

According to authentic records published by the leading newspapers of Marion, Carbondale, and Carterville, 1200 homes were destroyed or damaged in Murphysboro, and more than two hundred people were killed there, with property damage of $3,000,000.00. There were one hundred seventy-seven homes destroyed in DeSoto, seventy deaths reported, and one hundred seventy-five injured. In West Frankfort one hundred and ten were killed, five hundred injured and nine hundred twenty-five homes damaged or destroyed.

The military and relief work was well organized, which produced help in manpower, money, and supplies. The National Director of Red Cross disaster work said he had never witnesed such complete devastation and suffering, nor a disaster that embraced such a wide range of territory. War veterans likened it to the battlefields of France.

Our neighboring towns of Hurst and Bush were damaged greatly with twenty-four deaths and eighteen injuries.

In May, 1926, a lesser tornado struck Carterville, cutting

a wide swathe from the southwest near Oakwood Cemetery to Pea Ridge on the northeast. The Rice and Scoby greenhouse on Elles Avenue was completely demolished, and many homes were extensively damaged. Fortunately, there were no casualties.

Woodlands

There were two big woods that fit in with the history of the town. The one at the south corporate limits was Horn's woods and is now entirely extinct. I do not know whether the inventor David Horn of Horn's-Go-Devil (previously mentioned) was the original owner or not. I do recollect, however, from my early childhood, going there to an Easter-egg hunt sponsored by the Methodist Sunday School. Children and young people looked forward each spring to walk through it searching for wild flowers, which was an afternoon's recreation. The woods as I remember was dense with big trees —no doubt many of them virgin timber. Later Monroe Brann obtained this tract; the trees were felled for his saw mill. It is said, too, that sometimes gypsies camped in it.

Bordering the east side of North Division Street near the city limits, the Burr Woods stretched eastward to the old streetcar line. It takes its name from the Old Burr mine which was the first deep-shaft mine sunk at Carterville on what was known as the Mary Peterson farm near the woods. There was a road leading through this woodland to the powder house and on to the mine. It is still quite a large wooded area, and there is evidence of many cave-holes yet.

Often in summer gypsies pitched their tents or parked their wagons, setting up camp and tethering their horses in the cool shade. I have seen the gaudily dressed women and girls on many occasions as they went from house to house in our part of town peddling handmade rustic chairs, settees, stools, or small tables fashioned from the willow branches and hickory which were freely available. This type of rustic furniture was

167

quite attractive and would be designated as patio furniture now.

In discussing the life of the gypsies, Jean Jones has given me a true story. Once a gypsy woman came to her Aunt Eva Burkholder's home just north of the woods and wanted to borrow a tub and get water out of the well there for her white horse. She said she didn't want her horse to drink the muddy branch water nearby. Mrs. Burkholder let her draw a tub full from the well. Later the woman proved her honesty by returning the zinc tub, which refutes the common belief in those days that gypsies could not be trusted. Most everyone thought gypsies were crafty with fortune-telling, and also swindlers, and townspeople did not welcome their presence.

At the north extremity of the Burr Woods was a beautiful, substantial two-story house where the parents of Charles and Marion Bush lived—later the Upshaw family. Mrs. Bush kept boarders. Today there are several modern homes, both brick and frame, at the edge of the woods facing this section of Division Street.

Concerning G. A. R. and John A. Logan

In 1881, Carterville Post No. 237, G.A.R. (Grand Army of the Republic) was chartered and by 1887 had a membership of thirty-eight. The town was proud of the veterans who had fought in the Civil War to save the Union. Many of them had heard General John A. Logan make his famous speech at the courthouse in Marion that influenced scores to volunteer in the service of their country. Jehu Beavers was one of them. I remember an enlarged picture of Logan in his home, also a battle-scarred flag that was carried on Sherman's March to the Sea. This flag years later was given to the State of Illinois for repository. Uncle Jehu, as he was known in his elder years, lived in our neighborhood and often came to our home in my teenage years. I wish now I had taken down notes of some of the experiences he related. Civil War songs were sung at our "Opening Exercises" during elementary and high-school days, and we loved to sing songs that were "Tenting Tonight," "Marching through Georgia," "Dixie," and "When Johnny Comes Marching Home Again."

Uncle Jehu's youngest son, Jim, was quite witty. On one occasion while he, his wife Nellie and I were sitting on their porch, one of his neighbors came riding by in a Model-T Ford. In the back seat of the car was the mother, looking so relaxed and calm that Jim remarked, "Look, there goes Mrs. A. She's suffering satisfaction."

Homespun Wit

Another incident stands out concerning Mr. and Mrs. Jerry Deason, well-known and much-respected residents. Mrs. Deason told this story herself when attending the Ladies' Aid one Thursday afternoon. While at a previous "Aid" meeting her husband had gone down into their cistern to give it a periodic cleaning—no city water then. She was a very meticulous person, a perfect housekeeper and a fine dressmaker. Her three daughters, Mae, Pearl, and Hazel, always were dressed beautifully. On arriving home that afternoon, she climbed down the ladder into the cistern and proceeded to clean it her way. Mr. Deason promptly ascended the rungs and pulled the ladder up after him, letting her stay down there until she sweated her dissatisfaction out.

"Bits and Wits" about Italian Emmigrants and Peddlers

M. W. Sizemore and Leo Watson during their early banking days served many Italian miners from Dewmaine and Colp who needed money orders written out for them to send back to their families in Italy. One, Polyfroni Sylvester, small of stature, was always smiling when he came into the Carterville State and Savings Bank. On his final visit he wanted to withdraw his savings in order to return to the "Old Country." As a parting thought, Mr. Sizemore remarked, "In case we don't see each other again, I wish you well." To which the Italian responded with his hands pointing upward, "Me see you upstairs."

Leo wrote most of the money orders for these people; and he told me he remembered also Roco Polito, a big husky fellow who came in the bank most every payday. Leo always would ask him how he felt, and his answer every time was, "Juice the same! Juice the same!"

Russel Crain, a prominent young man employed in the Elles Store here in the early 1900's, desired to be helpful to some Italian women who had come to the store early and were turning the bundles of cloth remnants over and over as well as upside down. Their English was very broken, and Russell was enjoying their curiosity in searching the bargains on the big table. Finally, sort of exasperated at their slowness in making selections, he picked up a bundle and said, "Here is a good one! Can't you smell the ocean on it?"

Two local men, Clate Brown and Pete Baker, would bring fire-kindlers to the bank and always ask Leo, "Would you like to buy any today? They're gooduns." I remember Pete Baker as a janitor at the old North Side School about the time I was a fourth-grader. He always loved to entertain the children playing his Jew's harp around the pot-bellied stove.

An Italian woman peddler known as "Sicilian Mary" made her rounds for several summers carrying a heavy canvas, strapped valise and wearing woolen coats. The valise was bulging with fine linens, tablecloths, napkins and hand-drawn scarves. Once she came to our home right at noontime. The day was beastly hot. Mama invited her to eat with us. She did, and to show her gratitude, she gave my mother a very beautiful, big tablecloth—white and blue border, pure linen.

There was the usual "Junk Man" who drove a one-horse wagon over town. The boys especially looked forward to his coming, many having gathered up all kinds of rags, tin, scrap iron and bottles to sell for even just a pretty penny. My father had a record he played on our Victor talking machine which we enjoyed hearing. The words went like this:

Any rags, any bones, any bottles today?
It's the same old story in the same old way.
A-N-Y R-A-G-S!

There were two men who were never known to curse but
had developed by-words of their own. Sam Carlisle's choice
words were "The devil and hell" when he became aggravated.
Alvin Lowry's familiar saying was "Dad blime it!"

Musical composers were known to go from house to house,
especially where there was an upright piano and young people taking music lessons. G. B. Fields of Fairfield, Illinois
was that type of music peddler. I still have three of composi-
tions, both words and music, that my mother bought, and
they, no doubt, were inspirational in creating in me a love
of history. The titles and dates copyrighted are:

"Our Fallen Chief" (McKinley—1901—dedicated to our
assassinated President).

"Flood of Shawneetown" (1898—dedicated to C. R. Gal-
loway, who lost a wife and two daughters in the great disaster,
April 3, 1898).

"Burning of the Iroquois Theatre" (1904—dedicated to the
brave comedian Eddie Foy).

Another historical sheet of music which I have kept is
"You Flew Over: Uncle Sam Takes His Hat off to You." It
was written in 1927 and dedicated to Captain Charles Lindbergh and *The Spirit of St. Louis.*

Strange Ordinances

In *The City of Carterville, Revised Laws and Ordinances,
1920,* I have discovered several that would seem odd today,
such as "whoever shall appear upon the streets or any public
place within the city in a dress not belonging to his or her
sex . . . shall be fined not less than three dollars nor more than
two hundred dollars. Provided that this section shall not apply
to the celebration of Halloween, national holidays, or other
public events.

171

"... at the hour of 8 o'clock P.M. each day the police shall cause to be sounded the fire bell, or cause to be blown the fire whistle . . . to be known as the "curfew," after which it shall be unlawful for any person under fourteen years of age to be on the streets of the city unless accompanied by parents.

". . . spitting on sidewalk forbidden. . . . Fine to be imposed not less than one dollar, nor more than ten dollars.

"Hours for cleaning privies—No privy or privy vault shall be opened nor the contents disturbed before the hour of 9 o'clock P.M. nor after 4 o'clock A.M.

"The city scavenger charge for removing slop per 10-gallon can: .15c. For cleaning residence privies: .50c. For removing dry garbage per barrel: .25c. For removing wet garbage and cinders per wagonload: 1.00. Penalty for refusing to pay, not less than $5.00 nor more than $200.00.

"Speed limit for automobiles, motor vehicles or motorcycle upon any streets in the city unlawful at a greater speed than ten miles an hour."

It is to be noted that hog pens were allowed in the early days and slop cans were common. The scavenger was jokingly referred to as "the honey-dipper man", a name some wit in town had concocted.

How times have changed!

Famous People

Throughout this narrative, several very famous people have been mentioned who have come to Carterville or within its proximity. Others in these afterthoughts should be in this story.

In was during the early part of the Depression that Mrs. Eleanor Roosevelt made a visit to Colp and went down in Madison No. 9 coal mine. Maxine Walker has related this to me. The choir of the Negro church sang for her. The First Lady was so impressed with their harmonious music, she later sent to them lovely maroon-colored robes with white stoles. That spring this fine choir, known as the Roland

172

Hayes singers, was invited to sing at the Southern Illinois Divisional Teacher's Meeting in Shryock Auditorium at the University in Carbondale. The choir director gave public acknowledgement in appreciation to the President's wife for this gift. I learned, too, that Roland Hayes was regarded at that time the most famous singer of his race. I recommend the book *Angel Mo and Her Son Roland Hayes* for the complete story.

John F. Kennedy came to our nearby Williamson County Airport in 1960.

Former President Dwight D. Eisenhower landed at the same airport October 28, 1962, being welcomed by Senator Everett Kirksen and committee at that time.

For our Illinois Sesquicentennial parade in September, 1968, Congressman Kenneth Gray flew in by helicopter and headed the parade formed at our high school.

A surprise "whistle stop" was made by Julie Nixon and David Eisenhower by train, stopping at the intersection of Division Street and Grand Avenue in the interest of her father's campaign for President in 1968. He later visited the Williamson County Airport.

Going back fifty years, I remember a son-in-law of William Jennings Bryan exhibited a large painting of his interpretation of "The Lord's Supper" which was set up all across the south interior wall of the J. J. Hunter building. Mr. Crisenberry promoted its showing, and I believe most of the high-school and grade-school students went to see it for a very reasonable price. The artist's name was Owen, and he was at that time the husband of Ruth Bryan, daughter of the "Great Commoner." Viewing this massive painting deepened our appreciation of art.

A Notable Pioneer

I feel I must insert a brief account of Abe Fowler that links in with the story of Carterville. In 1845, driving a yoke of oxen, he came from Alabama, settling on a farm southwest of here. The log cabin he built was removed in 1939 in clearing territory for Crab Orchard Lake. In young manhood he built a beautiful two-story frame house with a huge barn nearby, both on the tract of land on which in 1968 the Shawnee Library System Administrative Headquarters was erected. The house burned several years ago, and the barn was torn down. The oxen yoke, incidentally, is now treasured by "Uncle Abe's" grandson, Frank Sherman Myers, as is also the bayonet Mr. Fowler had carried through the entire Civil War as a loyal Union soldier under the leadership of General Logan. He had also endured the suffering and hardships in the infamous Andersonville Prison.

The John A. Logan Junior College is just across the road east of the impressive Shawnee Library System Building. Much more could be told about both of these educational institutions, but that is a story some future historian will relate.

Suffice it to say, I feel sure few old-timers now living ever dreamed that Carterville, which in its young days was nationally known as a coal mining town, would by 1970 become a college town. With this new junior college also S.I.U. Vocational Technical Institute and the wonderful book-distributing center provided by the Shawnee Library System, serving thirty-three libraries in eighteen counties of Southern Illinois, plus the fine recreational facilities at nearby Lake Crab Orchard, it is now rated as the fastest-growing city in this end of the state.

Life's rear-view mirror—memory—inevitably becomes more interesting as the years roll. We should enjoy looking back over the road we have travelled—and pause and reflect on the significant things that have happened to Carterville these one hundred years past!

EPILOGUE

Someone has said, "You really see your town when you know you belong to it."

When I retired from Welfare work in 1961, I told my co-workers that I desired to spend some of my free time in writing of experiences in my life. But leisure has been limited in my case, for I assumed a third career! Our small library needed a librarian in 1964, and I volunteered to assume this responsibility and promote its growth. Receiving many requests for historical information about Carterville, of which there is a dearth, I became intensely interested in collecting data to compile a sort of human-interest history of our small town that was approaching its centennial year. It has truly been a labor of love; and if in this story I have been able to bring to light a portion of Carterville's unique history, I shall feel this will be a living memorial as my own contribution in community service to the town where I was born and where I have resided all my life.

Now I know I belong to it!

BIBLIOGRAPHY

History of Gallatin, Saline, Hamilton, Franklin and Williamson Counties, Illinois: 1887—Goodspeed Publishing Company.

Historical Souvenir of Williamson County, Illinois: 1905—
H. F. Wilcox.

History of Southern Illinois, 1912—George W, Smith.

Williamson County Illinois in the World War, 1917-1918—
Hal W. Trovillion.

Revised Laws and Ordinances of the City of Carterville—
1920.

Pioneer Folks and Places—Barbara Burr Hubbs.

Souvenir Program, Williamson County Centennial, 1939.

Williamson County Fair Homecoming, 100th Aniversary,
1856-1956.

The Black Diamond, C. H. S., 1925.

Stirring Lives of Buffalo Bill and Pawnee Bill—Frank C.
Cooper.

Looking at 100 Years First Baptist, Herrin, Illinois—Mabel
McNeill.

University Museum, Southern Illinois University—J. Charles
Kelley.

This Fabulous Century, 1870-1900—Time-Life Books.

History of the First Baptist Church of Carterville—Cavanas
Scoby.

Illinois History, Vol. 21, Number 1, October 1967, "World's
Worst Tornado," by Randy Moore.

The Carterville Herald, January 17, 1919.

The Carterville Herald, October 6, 1922.

The Carterville Herald, February 27, 1931.

The Carterville Herald, April 7, 1944.

The Carterville Herald, April 1, 1948
The Carterville Herald, July 2, 1954.
The Carterville Herald, July 9, 1954.
The Carterville Herald, April 19, 1957.
The Carterville Herald, June 14, 1957.
Encyclopedia Americana, Vol. 7, 1956.